TANNI

TANNI

TED HARRISON

CollinsWillow

An Imprint of HarperCollins*Publishers*

First published in 1996
by CollinsWillow
an imprint of HarperCollins*Publishers*
London

1 3 5 7 9 10 8 6 4 2

A CIP catalogue record for this book is
available from the British Library

ISBN 0 00 218723 X

Origination by Colourscan

Printed and bound by
Caledonian International Book Manufacturer

PICTURE ACKNOWLEDGEMENTS
The publishers would like to thank the following sources:
Allsport, Dinah Cadogan, Tanni, Peter and Sulwen Grey,
Mark Shearman, the *Western Mail* and *South Wales Echo*

Contents

Acknowledgements

IN WRITING THIS book about Tanni, the first people I must thank are her family, Peter and Sulwen Grey – her parents, and her sister Sian. Throughout they have been immensely helpful and willing to talk about both the happy as well as the difficult times, with equal honesty and candour.

My thanks too go to Tanni's friends, fellow competitors and the many others who have played an important part in shaping her life. Special mention should perhaps be made of Mrs Gill Thomas who died just days after recording her memories as one of Tanni's most influential teachers.

The book would not have taken shape anything like as efficiently without the help of my daughter Caroline who was also much involved in the research.

Thanks also go to those in the Willow department at HarperCollins*Publishers*, to Monica Chakraverty for editing the book and to designer Rachel Smyth.

And co-operating with Tanni herself has been a great delight. It must be very odd seeing one's life story being turned into a permanent record for a wider readership. But Tanni appears to have been unfazed by the process and patient with all the demands.

Introduction

*'It's not what you have lost,
but what you have left that counts.'*
Sir Ludwig Guttmann, founder of the Paralympic Games

*T*ANNI GREY IS a world-class athlete. In 1992 she returned from the Olympic city of Barcelona with more medals than any other British female competitor.

Today, in this era of air travel and sports sponsorship, Tanni travels the world competing in games, exhibition events and road races as one of the élite – a full-time and dedicated sports-woman. She also needs to follow a demanding, rigorous and carefully monitored specialist training schedule which includes muscle building, race practice and extending her stamina.

She is additionally a celebrity in Britain, especially in her home country of Wales where she is an ambassador for her sport and on the international scene she is a high-profile role model. She has received some of the United Kingdom's most prestigious sports awards. Her vivacious personality is familiar on radio and television.

The only difference between Tanni and most other leading sports personalities is that Tanni, since childhood, has not had the use of her legs. Her sport is wheelchair racing, a relatively new event, which in recent years has advanced at considerable speed, thanks to the production of ultra light high-tech racing chairs and the emergence of a corp of élite athletes.

In an earlier age, despite her personality and determination, Tanni would probably have been destined to live a low-profile, unfulfilling life as a disabled person. In some cultures because of her congenital disability, spina bifida, she might even have been kept out of sight in the family home.

Fortunately for Tanni she grew up at a time when the Paralympic movement was coming of age. Originally the movement had been conceived as therapy for young people, in particular the war-wounded, who had lost the use of their lower limbs through spinal injury.

Then it evolved into a movement to give people with other disabilities the opportunities of taking part in competitive games. Yet, until recently according to Tanni, it was still viewed by many people as a sideshow to the real thing. 'The cripples doing their brave best.'

The emergence however of élite sportsmen and women challenged this notion. In wheelchair-racing in particular it is possible for Paralympians to train in the same manner as their able-bodied colleagues in other sports. Theirs is an event where disabilities are discounted.

It is generally accepted that sportsmen and women select the events which best suit their physique. A six foot eight inch Harlem Globetrotter cannot expect to win the Derby as a jockey. A champion jockey would be unrealistic in the extreme if he or she expected to join a top basketball team. Athletes who, for whatever reason, find their legs are of little use, can nevertheless develop their upper bodies and hone their tactical skills to excel at wheelchair-racing, a sport which, judging from the enthusiasm of the tens of thousands of people who packed the Barcelona stadium in 1992, provides great spectator value.

Their sports chairs are viewed by the athletes as machines on a par with bicycles and the parallels between wheelchair-racing and cycling are close. Both rely on similar developments in technology and sports science. The only essential difference between the two disciplines is that, in common with other Paralympic sports, wheelchair athletes are classified according to their disabilities to enable them to compete with each other on equal terms.

There are four basic classifications determined by the way the athletes' bodies function. Someone with a damaged spine towards the neck has less ability to control balance and diminished power in the upper arms than someone with damage much lower down the spinal column. Classification, of course, is not unique to the Paralympic movement and is widely accepted in certain other sports. A flyweight boxer would never be matched against a heavyweight, for instance.

Spina bifida or *rachischisis* is a condition which comes in many degrees of severity. Essentially, it involves a failure of the back bone and spinal cord to develop completely. Exactly why this happens in the womb is not fully understood. This malformation can in turn lead to paralysis of the muscles below the lesion and the degree of disability depends both on the nature of the spinal malformation and the position it occurs on the spine. In some cases a baby can be born with the entire spinal cord exposed, in other less severe cases the cord is protected by tissue and skin.

Tanni's classification is T3, which means that damage to her spine is low in the back and she has full use of her arms, shoulders and torso. She competes not only in this category, but frequently against those classified as T4, who should in theory be at a physical advantage, and often she beats them.

Tanni Grey has been at the forefront of wheelchair racing and the Paralympic movement for eight years. In many ways she has been responsible for lifting the status of the sport by being seen as a dedicated sportswoman in her own right. Her story, however, is not one of easy achievement. Vital to her success has been the fact that she was born to unusually determined and forward-thinking parents. Throughout her childhood, she and her parents have had to battle against the attitudes of society and authority. And through the story of her life it can be seen how attitudes to disability have changed and are changing but still have a long way to go.

CHAPTER ONE

A tiny thing

'…it did not occur to me that I was any different.'

'SHE'S DEAD … she must be dead.'

Exhausted after six-and-a-half hours in labour, this was the only conclusion that made sense to Sulwen. Minutes had gone by and still she had not been allowed to see her baby.

'Is the baby in the nursery?' she asked her husband Peter.

'No,' he replied, 'she's in an incubator.'

'Why?' Sulwen demanded suspiciously. 'She's dead, isn't she?'

From the little information he had gleaned, Peter Grey tried to reassure his wife. Immediately after the birth, their child had been rushed away from the delivery room by the medical staff at the Glossop Maternity Hospital in Cardiff and Peter had been told to go to a waiting room. It was not what he had been expecting. Nearly two years earlier when Sian, his first daughter, had been born things had been very different. The labour had been much longer but, just after the birth, the new baby, wrapped and cleaned, was placed in her father's arms.

On this occasion however he was left waiting anxiously for news. Before long the duty doctor came to speak to him and said that the baby had spina bifida. This was not a term that meant anything to Peter, but then the doctor added words that Peter has never forgotten, 'If your name was down to have a spina bifida child, then you can get down on your knees and thank God'. Meaning, of course, that they should be thankful that their daughter's spina bifida was a mild case – Peter was to learn quite soon that the deformity could have been much worse.

The doctor then took Peter to the intensive care unit where he saw his daughter, in all the after-shock of birth, lying in an incubator. She weighed six-and-a-half pounds and was a straggly nineteen-and-a-half inches long. As Peter stood looking down at her, the doctor gently turned her over. There on the lower part of her back was the tell-tale lump from which the diagnosis had been made. 'It looked,' Peter said, 'like half a boiled egg, but covered with perfect skin.'

Then Peter became aware that the doctor was trying to show him some of the other children in the unit.

'They were all struggling for life.' he said. 'There were kids with sunken and inverted chests. It was an eye-opener' I realized then what the doctor had meant. This is what Tanni could have been like.'

When Peter returned to Sulwen he had just the bare minimum of knowledge, but enough to convince his wife that the worst had not happened. Their baby was not dead. She had been born with spina bifida. What exactly that meant and what it would mean over the years they had no idea.

Later that morning Sulwen had a chance to ask more. One question she distinctly remembers asking the doctors was would her new daughter, in time, be able to have children of her own? That, to her, seemed a yardstick of normality.

'They told me, "yes, she will be able to have children". I clung to that thought, convinced that if that was the case things could not be too bad. I don't know if they just said it to pacify me. '

At that moment Sulwen had still not seen her daughter. All that she knew was that there was something wrong with her, something labelled spina bifida and that Peter had explained that the baby had 'a little bump on her back like a blister'.

When it came to her first glimpse of the baby, Sulwen now feels that the medical staff lacked both sympathy and understanding. When a mother sees her disabled child for the first time it is a traumatic and emotional experience.

'It would have been so much better had I been able to go with Peter, or even with a nurse, but the medical staff just left me to go on my own. I went to the unit and saw this long straggly baby in an incubator, no hair, little sticking-out ears and a bump on the back which was so much bigger than I had expected. It was a shock because, in my mind, I had visualized something very small. The second shock was not being allowed to pick her up. She had to stay in the incubator.'

On the Monday, when the little baby was just two days old, it was decided that she had to be taken for a detailed examination at the Cardiff Royal Infirmary nearby. She was to have X-rays of the kidney and bladder and, prior to that, was not allowed to have anything to drink.

'The baby was beside herself with hunger and thirst.' Sulwen recalls. 'I knew she was crying and screaming, even though the nurses kept telling me she was all right. But when it's your own child, you can tell. It was then that I really began to grieve for her. I was surrounded by people who had got perfect babies and something was wrong with mine. The approach of the hospital could certainly have been more understanding. It seemed a little hard at the time.'

Despite the shock and confusion of discovering that their new daughter had been born with what the medical profession sees as an 'abnormal condition' and the insensitivity of the medical system, there was also joy and delight at the birth of Carys Davina at 1.25 am on Saturday, 26 July 1969. Peter chose the two names – Carys because it is a traditional Welsh name which he understood meant 'beloved', and Davina because it is Sulwen's middle name.

Four days later, after the detailed medical examination, Carys was on her way home to the house in St Alban's Avenue, in the Cardiff suburb of Heath in South Wales, where her parents had lived all their married life. There her elder sister, Sian, saw the new baby for the first time.

Sian too had had an upsetting few days. At the age of less than two years when mother disappears, if only for five days, it can seem like an eternity. Sian had spent many hours standing at the front door crying and waiting for her mother to return. However, when Sulwen returned with the new baby that was all in the past. The main thing now for Sian was to get to know a sister, a major event in any child's life. It was not long after seeing Carys for the first time, having inspected her closely and perhaps having expected something larger, that she declared how tiny the baby was. From that moment, for Sian and the rest of the family Carys became known as Tiny, a nickname which quickly developed into Tanni. And the name stuck.

Tanni's consultant orthopaedic surgeon, Mr Hanus Weisl, describes Tanni's condition as 'closed' spina bifida. Twenty-five years ago he recalls seeing two or three new cases every week in South Wales where he worked, but today his successors see perhaps only one or two children with the condition a month. A key reason for this is that it is now possible to diagnose spina bifida at a very early stage in pregnancy and for parents to be offered the option of a termination.

Obviously this is a sensitive area for many adults with spina bifida who realize that in some instances, had early diagnosis been possible in their day, their parents might have chosen for them never to have been born.

Today, as an adult, Tanni knows that these are questions that she may one day need to face for herself. She is however a character who prefers to cross bridges when she comes to them rather than to ponder and worry unnecessarily about hypothetical questions and situations.

'In one sense,' she says, 'it would be easy for me to think and feel as most able-bodied people do that I would not want to bear a disabled child. But how would I react? After all, I do not really think of myself as disabled.

'I know that my mum has said that if she had had a test and been warned that I was disabled, she probably would have had an abortion. But that was before I was born, before she knew me. I wasn't Tanni then. So I can accept that there are women who do not want to have a child with a disability.'

Knowing what her mother might have done has not in any way altered Tanni's love and regard for her mother. She shrugs off the 'what if?' questions of life and, when pressed, adds, 'If I had been aborted I would not have known anything about it. So what is the point in getting worked up or angry about something I would not have known?'

Tanni then turns the discussion in a different direction. She points to the way severely disabled children who would have died in infancy are now kept alive by medical science. Should they be kept alive? she asks, offering no answer of her own, for like most people she has no answer. Then, as an afterthought, she adds: 'There would be lots of advantages for a disabled kid to have a mother like me. I would know more than most parents about how to raise him or her.'

It is a subject she bats around with the detachment of a student in a philosophy seminar, but refuses to consider in too deep a personal way. 'Who knows, I may never be able to have or even want children.'

Sulwen confirms that if she had known that she was carrying a disabled child and had been given the option, she would have had an abortion.

'I think it is wrong to *knowingly* bring a disabled child into the world,' she says, 'because of the pressures it can put on a family. Although some women would be horrified and worried that there would be a stigma attached to having a disabled child, that is not my concern. I would not be worried about a disabled child affecting my image or putting a stop to the things I wanted to do. I look at it from the point of view that, at some point, a disabled child could be left for someone else to look after.

'If I had had an abortion I would not have known anything about Tanni, not even if she was a boy or a girl. At that stage, I would have believed it better to have an abortion and have another go. Having said that, there has never been one second since Tanni was born that I have ever wished I had had an abortion. I've torn my hair out with her, but that has nothing to do with her disability!'

As to why Tanni was born with spina bifida, Sulwen has no answers.

'There are so many stories and theories. One is that mothers whose parents are old are at risk. My mother was forty when I was born and my father forty-nine. So that theory would fit me. But then I heard it was caused by not eating enough greens or eating bad potatoes. Well, I had a normal diet. You never think you are going to have a disabled child and there is always a big question mark hanging over life when it happens.'

In its most serious form spina bifida – a congenital defect described by the medical profession as a non-union of one or more vertebral arches – can also cause severe brain damage and spasticity and liver and kidney complications. Mr Weisl is now retired but, looking back over years in which he met and treated hundreds of children with spina bifida, he observes that what really makes a difference to a child in the long term is not the precise nature of the spina bifida but 'what happens in their head'.

'If these kids maintain their IQ, they do reasonably well. What really matters is not how bad the spina bifida is, but what sort of person they are.'

The most immediate implication for Tanni and her parents was that the hospital required her to come for regular check-ups. There were orthopaedic, spina bifida and neurology clinics to attend. In typical fashion each medical specialization wanted to be involved. Sulwen noticed a particular interest in measuring Tanni's head. Still not fully aware of the full meaning of spina bifida, it was only later that Sulwen realized that this careful procedure was to check to see if Tanni was developing hydrocephalus, the alarming and, until recently, potentially fatal condition in which excessive quantities of fluid from the spine build up in the brain. This can be one of the consequences of spina bifida and the heads of children with the condition swell to a disproportionate size.

Peter and Sulwen were learning as they went along. If they had known all the potential problems they admit now they would have worried a great deal more. Sulwen feels that she would have become obsessed with the idea that Tanni's head might have been expanding with hydrocephalus and would have measured it constantly. Peter might have reflected more on his one-and-only contact with the condition a few years earlier when he had seen a young child in a hospital ward which he was visiting in his professional capacity as an architect.

'There was a boy in a bed with a head, as I remember it, the size of his body. This was before the days of the shunt, the procedure they can now use to drain fluid off the brain. I asked what would happen to him and was told that one day there would just be a red bed because his head would have exploded.'

Extreme cases of hydrocephalus can now be averted but, fortunately for Tanni, her spina bifida did not develop into it. For the first years of her life, despite the condition, she developed as any other baby – growing, learning, experimenting, laughing and crying in all the usual ways. Ironically it was not Tanni but her sister who first needed treatment for a serious medical condition. It was noticed that Sian was walking awkwardly. She had been limping for a while but it was thought she was just finding it difficult to get around in bulky nappies. The staff at the spina bifida clinic, however feared that Sian might have an internal or invisible spina bifida but, on examining her, they found that she had a dislocated hip.

Soon Sian was in hospital and spent six weeks in traction. Then, once the ball-and-socket joint was in place, she was covered in plaster. She was only two at the time and could only speak in baby talk. She was to remain in plaster for eighteen months. But that was not all. She had hardly been out of hospital for two weeks when she developed a cold on her chest and, in the course of a normal examination of her chest, the local GP, Dr David Richards, heard a heart murmur through his stethoscope.

Sian was referred to a specialist cardiac paediatrician who diagnosed the congenital condition *patent ductus arteriosus*. This involves a failure of a blood vessel, active in a child before birth, to close after delivery. It results in blood circulating without having passed through the lungs to be oxygenated. If untreated a patient with this condition is unlikely to live into adulthood.

It was recommended that Sian be operated on as soon as she came out of plaster and this would have happened as planned but for another ill chance. Shortly after Sian was liberated from her plaster cast the family took a brief holiday in the course of which Sian broke her leg and was back in plaster for another eight weeks.

In the end the operation did take place. Today the procedure would most likely involve micro-surgery with the surgeon gaining access to the site from the groin via a blood vessel. In Sian's case she was opened up by a major incision and still has the scar. Nevertheless the operation was a success.

For Sulwen and Peter Grey there was little respite from medical matters. Sian was now walking well and her heart condition corrected, but Tanni was beginning to show the early signs of disability.

For many parents it is very difficult to understand, amidst their own anxieties, how their children are feeling when they are taken over by the medical system. Peter however was in a better position than many to appreciate what was going on in his daughter's mind. He too had had a childhood bedevilled by ill health. He was born with what in the 1930s was known as 'knock knee' and, until the age of seven, his legs had been kept in irons. Following an operation he developed diphtheria in hospital and then on his return home it was decided that his tonsils and adenoids needed to be removed. This was done in a way not unusual at the time, on the dining room table, with the operation being carried out by the local doctor, who anaesthetized him with gas through a suffocating rubber mask.

'At the end of the operation,' Peter said, recounting a family story, 'the doctor lost the tonsils and it was thought that the cat had swiped them, until he eventually found them!'

Then, at the age of seven, it was found that Peter was experiencing epilepsy, having up to forty *petit mal* attacks a day. These attacks involve just a brief loss of concentration or consciousness and, in most cases, the patient does not go into a fit but simply appears to be thinking deeply.

As a result of this childhood history Peter developed a philosophy towards his daughters which was, especially in Tanni's case, to have far-reaching consequences.

'Having had it ingrained into me that there were so many things I could not and should not do because of my health, I came to be a firm believer in the saying that in life one is never given a cross greater than you can bear. Nothing is given you in life that you cannot cope with. What you get out of the experience is another matter and up to you. So I've always encouraged my own children to take opportunities in life. I am aware that, for a variety of reasons, doors opened for me and I didn't go through them. But with Tanni when an opportunity arises I say, "go for it – try it". I put some pressure on her whereas I myself had tended just to sit back.'

Arguably it is from Peter Grey's side of the family that Tanni was to develop her competitiveness. Peter's father, Alex, had been a successful racing motorcyclist in the 1920s. He won the Welsh TT and Peter still has the silver cup on display. He was an amateur and would buy production machines and tune them to beat the works' bikes. He competed on the Isle of Man and it was there that he had an accident which put a stop to serious competition. He was flung as high as a telegraph pole and was saved from serious injury by his leathers and helmet. By the time Peter was born he had retired from the motor cycling scene. He died at the age of seventy-eight.

Peter's mother had come from Birkenhead but could trace her family to Lincolnshire where they had lived for generations in the 'Red House' on the old Roman Road the Fosse Way. Peter himself had been born in Cardiff in 1933 and South Wales had always been his home. It was there he went to school and later trained and worked as an architect, becoming a director of works in the health service.

He cannot however claim the same pure Welsh ancestry as his wife. Sulwen's mother had been born in Penarth and her father in Cardiff, with grandparents coming from Neath and Mid Wales.

Both Welsh and English were spoken at home, with her mother and grandmother conversing in the Celtic tongue, often with Sulwen replying in English whilst her father, who spoke the best Welsh of all the family, preferred to speak English. Like Peter, Sulwen was an only child. Her father was a transport manager with the Co-op, her maternal grandfather was a guard on the Great Western Railway and her father's father had moved through a variety of jobs, from butcher to coal trimmer. He had died at the age of forty-eight, leaving eleven children with Sulwen's father being the eldest boy.

Sulwen left school at the age of sixteen with one career in mind, to be a food technologist. She studied for the qualifications, the National Diploma and City and Guild's exams, and became so skilled at baking bread and scones and icing and decorating cakes that she was asked to produce items for display and exhibition.

From the age of nineteen until the birth of Sian when she was twenty-seven, Sulwen worked for Elkes Biscuits in Cardiff. Her position was work's chemist and her responsibilities were to test ingredients to ensure the consistency of the firm's output. The strength of flour, for instance, had to be tested because if it was too strong the biscuits would be too small and if it was too weak the biscuits would spread in size and not fit the packaging.

The first meeting of Peter Grey and Sulwen Jones can hardly be said to have come from the pages of a romantic novel. He, a young architect had been sent by his firm to plan a new laboratory and lavatory block at a biscuit factory. There he met the work's chemist and asked her how she wanted her new laboratory planned. Where did she want the sinks and where should the work-tops be placed? Would she prefer teak or an artificial plastic-type finish? She, taken by surprise as she had not been expecting the visit, had no answers prepared and must, she feels, have appeared indecisive.

Romance however was in the air, for Peter decided to break his rule of not mixing work and pleasure and asked Sulwen if she would like to go out with him that Thursday evening.

All the time Peter had been asking the technical questions, Sulwen's mind had been spinning with other thoughts. She was wondering if this architect was married and concluded he must be. She even conjured up a mental image of a small, blonde wife.

'All this was going on while I was supposed to be deciding what I wanted in the laboratory. And then he asked me if I would like to go out with him and suggested Thursday. I explained I was working on Thursday. "Where will you be working?" he asked.

'"Here", I said, "I'm supervising a late shift until ten o'clock."

'"Oh, that's all right, I'll see you outside at ten."

'I didn't really expect to see him again, but I told my mother about the architect who had asked me out for a drink at ten o'clock and, although I usually had to be in by eleven, she agreed that I could be late on this one occasion.

'When Thursday came he was outside waiting for me and we went to the only pub which was open until half-past ten, the Black Cock on top of Caerphilly mountain. I had a sweet Martini, Peter had a pint of Hancock's Home Brew.

'He asked me if I'd go out with him again on the Saturday and I said no, I'd already made arrangements with other friends. He asked about the following Saturday and again I said no, I had already made other plans. He suggested the Saturday after and I agreed. He told me later that if I'd turned him down a third time, he would have given up.'

That was October 1961 and soon Peter and Sulwen began to see each other regularly. Within a year the relationship had developed to the point where an engagement was the next appropriate stage. Yet by October 1962 no date had been fixed either for an official engagement announcement or a wedding.

'We were talking about getting engaged by Christmas, or perhaps by March, but then Peter decided to change his car instead and I wasn't deliriously happy about that,' Sulwen remembers.

'Then on a Thursday night, we went to a dance. I had a terrible cold. We met some friends who had become engaged and they asked us about our plans. "I've no idea," I replied.'

Perhaps having overheard this remark, Peter said rather casually to Sulwen on their way home that they might, some time at the weekend, have a look around the jeweller's shop, which his family had always dealt with, adding 'just to have a look … not to buy anything'.

The next day at breakfast Peter asked his father, Alex, for directions to the jeweller. Naturally his father wanted to know why he needed this information.

'Just to have a look at some rings,' he said, adding 'not to buy anything just at the moment.'

'What sort of ring does Sulwen want?' Alex asked.

'She quite likes sapphires and diamonds I think,' Peter said.

That morning Alex Grey went to the jeweller himself, coming back with eight diamond rings on approval. When Peter came home at lunchtime the rings were displayed on a plate.

As Sulwen's cold had kept her at home that day Peter went round to see her. He explained that his father had brought home some engagement rings and Sulwen could choose one. He then went into the kitchen to see Sulwen's father to ask formally if he could marry his daughter. Mr Jones just continued to dry the dishes and said very little, but he gladly gave his consent.

Sulwen was unsure as to whether she should go to Peter's house to choose a ring. After all, if she was not well enough to go to work she could hardly be seen to be leaving the house. However with her mother's agreement she went round to see Peter's parents and was shown the rings.

Being of a thrifty Welsh nature and seeing the price tags she realized that even the cheapest one was twice the price that Peter had wanted to pay. She tried them all on and chose the least expensive.

'Are you sure?' Peter asked, pointing to another, the second most expensive. 'Don't you like this one better?'

Of course she did, but she thought it polite to select one at the bottom end of the price range. However she tried the other ring on again and Peter said, 'If you like it, you might as well have it'.

And that was that. Sulwen went into the other room and

showed Peter's parents the ring and Alex Grey poured them all a glass of sherry.

'I had thought of spending perhaps £35 on a ring.' Peter remembers. 'It was all I thought I could afford, but my mother said I should think of paying more. If, she said, I wanted Sulwen to be proud of wearing my ring in thirty years time, when my position might be rather different, I should be prepared to dig a bit deeper.'

Thus it was that on 12 October 1962 Sulwen and Peter became engaged. Their wedding was held seventeen months later on 14 March 1964 at the Crwys Road Methodist Church where Sulwen had been christened. She had been born on Whit Sunday and her name, in the Welsh feminine form, means Whitsun.

A few weeks before the wedding Peter had joked that just before all the major events of his life he had been taken ill. He had gone down with chickenpox before one major set of exams, with measles before something else. What would he catch before the wedding? In the event the joke backfired. Peter went down with pneumonia.

In her mind's eye, Sulwen still has the vision of her bride-groom on their wedding day: 'He had no colour, he had cold sores and dark circles under his eyes. He looked as though a puff of wind would blow him over.'

The wedding however went ahead and, before long, the newly married couple moved in to the house in Heath where they live to this day and where both their children were brought up. It was the house that Peter's parents had bought some years before when Peter was a student and which they now sold to the newly-weds before moving themselves to a flat in another part of the city. As events turned out it was a fortuitous move, for the house was situated in one of the few areas of Cardiff where it is flat for half a mile in every direction. From the point of view of Tanni, in her formative years, there could not have been a better place for getting used to a wheelchair

Tanni's earliest memories are, typically, hazy images of inconsequential moments. She remembers being in a pram with a plastic teething ring, being pushed past the local chemist's shop. From an early age too she became very attached to a cuddly toy, a Christmas present which came to be called 'Red Baby'. Many years later in a magazine interview, she described Red Baby, somewhat tongue-in-cheek, as her first love. The worn and ragged toy survives and still lives on a top shelf gathering dust in Tanni's bedroom. It looks like a red teddy bear in body, but has the face of a doll. It is now held together with safety pins and its face is cracked, largely thanks to the day Sian threw it out of their bedroom window. Red Baby is truly hideous and truly much loved!

Tanni has snatches and episodes of memory of her early years which only become clear recollections from around the time when she started school. She clearly remembers the very first days of school, meeting new friends and discovering so many new things to do.

Like all parents, Sulwen and Peter Grey retain mental snap-shot recollections of their children when young. Sulwen can still see Tanni in their back garden at the age of three or four wearing a little poncho. Not that she was wearing it in the conventional way. She had lifted one corner up and had put it over her head like a hood. There she would sit, wearing a favourite pair of brown gloves, on an old log which to her and Sian was their car. Peter had given the log a steering wheel and a poker for a gear lever and there they would play turning the wheel and changing gear. Another make-believe game involved frying pretend chips by putting clothes pegs in a pan. And always there were the two family dogs – mother and daughter, Du and Pip – pottering around keeping an eye on the girls and especially protective of Tanni. Once on holiday two old ponies came wandering over to Tanni and Pip immediately warned them off, nipping one on the back for good measure. And, on another occasion in the snow, Pip raced out of the house to chase a neighbour's dog away from Tanni, knocking a snowman over in the process.

Like any sisters separated by little more than eighteen months Sian and Tanni played and fought. Until Tanni was thirteen they shared a bedroom. It was Tanni however, as Sulwen remembers it, who tended to be the bossy one and tried to order her elder sister around.

'I am not as competitive as Tanni,' Sian says, 'and I have always been less extroverted.'

It was when Tanni was about the age of five or six that she took a friend on an impromptu and totally unofficial house-to-house collection. They called on several neighbours' houses saying they were collecting money for blind children. When they returned to the friend's house with a tidy sum of money, the mother was so horrified that she made them take all the money back.

Around this time, when Tanni first went to school, it was noticed that she was having problems walking.

'Everything seemed so big,' she said, 'and it was difficult for me to walk so far. I would get tired very easily and fall down a lot. My friend, Sue Roberts, would hold my hand to stop me falling over and if I did take a tumble she would pick me up again.'

Thus it was that as she entered the world of school Tanni's spina bifida began to impinge on her life in a more significant way. Up until then her movements had been stiff and she had been more accident prone than other children of her age, but she had not been noticeably disabled.

'She did not have a great deal of control' Sulwen recounts. 'She was constantly falling over and always had plasters on her knees. If she went away from home, she'd come back with blood running down her legs. She also had to be very careful with her bladder because her paralysis was setting in from the waist down.'

What was happening was that, as Tanni grew, so greater pressure was put on the nerves in her spine. Sensation in the legs slowly dulled and, with increased body weight, her legs became less able to carry her.

When, in 1973, the time came for Tanni to start school Sulwen went to see the headmaster of Birchgrove primary school, just round the corner from their home. She explained to the headmaster, Mr Dewi Thomas, that Tanni had spina bifida and what that entailed. He, with a welcoming and enlightened view which was to be very important in Tanni's development, saw no problem in accepting her as a new pupil.

Despite starting school, the visits to the hospitals had to continue and it was decided at the spina bifida clinic that Tanni should be introduced to callipers. This was, initially, an unsuccessful experiment because, after a day, Tanni's legs began to blister. Sian vividly remembers being woken up in the night as Tanni's blisters appeared. It became apparent later that the brand new callipers should have been washed thoroughly before use, but no one in the health service had passed this information on. Tanni recalls being very excited about getting her first callipers and then very disappointed when the blisters developed. It was quite a while before she could wear them again.

'My legs were deteriorating quite badly,' she said, 'my ankles and my knees had given way. At the time I didn't really know what was happening because nobody really told me. It was much the same I believe for mum and dad. They had been told I had spina bifida and that was that. The hospital did not really explain what it was and what would happen.

'I just accepted that I had spina bifida, and I don't really remember anyone ever talking to me or explaining how my walking would get worse and I would end up in a wheelchair. Nobody ever told me and I never asked. It was only when I was older that I started questioning what the medical people were doing.'

'I've got vague recollections of Tanni walking and falling and cutting her knees,' says Sian. 'And I remember the blue buggy, the pushchair she had in case she got tired at school.'

Peter and Sulwen took each development as it came. They knew that they could turn up at the clinic at the Cardiff Royal Infirmary whenever they had a problem and that the staff were always willing to do their best. The trouble was no one knew exactly how Tanni's body would develop and if and when she would lose mobility. There was no danger that the damage to her spine would alter position and cause danger to a greater part of her body but what was not known was how severely the spina bifida might affect the lower part of the body from her lesion downwards.

Fortunately therefore, Tanni was not faced with the possibiltiy of the severest damage and hydrocephalus caused by the most damaging type of spina bifida. Her father must have frequently recalled the words of the doctor at Tanni's birth to 'thank God' that Tanni's was a relatively mild case.

'We knew what the future might hold and hoped it would never happen. The staff tried to boost our confidence and we in turn tried to boost Tanni's.' No-one kept anyone deliberately in the dark, it was just that there was nobody who could give a reliable prognosis.'

In due course a wheelchair was suggested and once again Mr Thomas willingly adapted to the changed circumstances. Most of the school was on the flat, and Sue or one of the stronger boys normally helped Tanni up the few steps to reach two classes that presented some access difficulties. Initially Tanni used the wheelchair as a back-up facility. She was encouraged to be as mobile as she could, using the wheelchair only when she was particularly tired or the terrain was difficult.

At Birchgrove Tanni was treated no differently from other pupils. As much was expected of her as was expected of her peers. Being bright and quick-witted, as her school reports testify, she did well academically.

Her report of February 1980, signed by Mr Thomas, refers to her continued progress and good work throughout the term. In all subjects from maths to Welsh, with the exception of art where her interest was adjudged to be only average, she was given a top classification. In the space reserved for special remarks she was said to be 'anxious to succeed and works hard'.

The only difference between Tanni and her schoolfriends was that occasionally Sulwen needed to be more involved than other mothers.

'If there was a school outing I was normally asked to go along to help push Tanni's buggy if necessary. Because Tanni also had a toileting problem I needed to be there and went on some very nice school trips!

'Tanni was accepted for who she was and I remember that one Christmas, because she couldn't walk across the stage, Tanni was the Christmas tree in the school play. She wore a big cape and stood on the stage with her callipers and zimmer frame.'

Her close friend Sue Roberts was big and strong for her age and very protective, as were Tanni's other friends. Sian, as can be the way with siblings, wanted little to do with her younger sister at school and they even made their own separate ways there each morning.

'Once Tanni and I were old enough to go to school by ourselves,' Sue Roberts recalls, 'I would come round to Tanni's house every morning and we would go together. She was very independent, but I could usually tell from her mood if she needed a helping hand.'

Today, Sue Roberts works for the South Glamorgan Health Authority in the Public Relations Department. She still keeps in touch with Tanni, although, thanks to Tanni's hectic lifestyle, getting together is difficult.

'I lived just round the corner and we played a lot together. We started infant's school at the same time, went through primary together, and saw a great deal of each other both in term and holidays. For example, we would organize games of tennis which we played on the road in front of her house.'

When the occasional playground insult came in Tanni's direction it was her gaggle of friends who leapt to her defence, especially Sue.

'There were a couple of kids, especially one girl who was a nasty character with everyone. She would wait until I was not around, and would then taunt Tanni about her disability. She got pleasure from doing think. She was jealous of Tanni's popularity and the attention she received. When I got to hear about her bullying, I would go ballistic!

'Tanni was upset by this girl and there were tears. She would wonder why she was being attacked for doing nothing wrong.'

There were also times when Tanni was away from her schoolfriends and became more sensitive to what others might think or say. Around the age of eight, she refused to attend the Girls' Brigade meetings at the local church when some of the other girls began calling her 'limpy legs'.

Today Tanni says that she only vaguely remembers these incidents.

'They must have got to me at the time but appear not to have done any lasting damage.'

Sulwen and Peter were aware that children of that age can often be very cruel. They knew that it took character and determination on Tanni's part to navigate her way successfully through her school days.

Tanni certainly learned how to cope with life and to take the knocks and her extroverted side began to develop. Looking in on the playground at Birchgrove Primary School at the time, outsiders would have seen Tanni very much at the centre of the noisiest gaggle of children waving her crutches around and directing operations.

'She would try everything,' says Sue, 'even the monkey bars in the playground. I would lift her up and she would swing along on her arms. She was extremely competitive.

'She certainly had a temper, but we never fell out for long. Some of this was frustration and being a placid person I would know when to back off and leave her be.'

Sian, too, talks of Tanni's short fuse. 'We have different temperaments. I take longer to reach an argument and then I sulk.'

Today the sisters are very different. 'I'm sure she's organized in a dis-organized way,' says Sian disparagingly but affectionately of Tanni.

'Sian,' Tanni retorts, is the sort of person who knows within two pence what she has in her bank account. She plans things months in advance while I arrange things the day before. She buys all the family Christmas presents and has usually done so by November.'

It was during one fierce argument between the two sisters that Tanni called Sian 'pig'. The nickname stuck. Sian responded by calling Tanni a slug.

The Grey family's next-door neighbours, Ivor and Eunice Clode (Uncle Ivor and Auntie Clode to Tanni) certainly recall the tantrums. 'She had a vicious temper,' said Ivor Clode, adding that he can still, in his mind's eye, see Tanni sitting on the floor screaming and shouting because 'something didn't suit her'. Or, as Sulwen puts it, echoing the thoughts of many mothers, 'There were a few times when I could have gladly strangled her!'

Ivor Clode, honourary uncle and godfather, adores Tanni. He has known both girls since they were born and has followed their careers with immense pride. 'Tanni's the extrovert, Sian's the thinker,' he says.

'From the start, Sulwen's reaction to Tanni's spina bifida was one of great determination. As far as she was concerned, Tanni wasn't disabled. We watched the way Tanni's condition changed over the years and saw her in crutches and then learning to use the wheelchair. But it never prevented her from joining in with everything. She was a good swimmer and at the pool would flop into the water like a seal, never wanting to be helped if possible.'

In 1980 when Tanni left Birchgrove School her time there was recognized by the teachers who presented her with a special plaque as a leaving gift. Inscribed on it were the words: 'Courage was the badge you wore with pride at Birchgrove Primary School'.

Peter and Sulwen display the plaque with pride in their living room, but Tanni herself has an ambivalent attitude towards it. She appreciates the good intentions behind its presentation, but now feels its presentation and inscription could be seen as expressing a certain attitude towards disabled people which Tanni would prefer to think of as belonging to the past. In other words, as much as the school had treated Tanni as just one of its many pupils, the fact that in the end a plaque had been presented to her suggests that they had viewed her as someone rather different or 'special'.

Among those attuned to the current political correctness of disability vocabulary, 'special' is an unacceptable word in that it is thought to imply a condescending separation of disabled people from the rest of the population. Back in 1980, of course, such thinking had not evolved and the presentation of the plaque to Tanni was an overwhelmingly popular move.

Yet even then Tanni was becoming aware of a gap between the way people perceived her and the way she perceived herself. When she joined friends in a fund-raising walk at the Maindy Stadium, she found that her contribution had been made the lead paragraph in the local newspaper report.

> *When Tania (sic) Grey, a Spina Bifida sufferer, completed two circuits of Maindy Stadium, the applause was reminiscent of a fine goal on the soccer field.*
>
> *The occasion was the annual sponsored walk for the Cardiff Schools' football league, and the effort by this young supporter from Birchgrove School typified the enthusiastic endeavour put into this venture by many people who cannot hope to 'star' in the game themselves.*

Tanni's recollection of this event is quite different. She went along with her friends in her normal matter-of-fact manner and did what she could in her callipers. She was surprised and somewhat annoyed at being made the centre of attention and receiving the rapturous applause.

It was one of those occasions when it occurred to her, although perhaps at the time she did not have the words to express it, that she was being patronized.

'The thing about Tanni,' Sue Roberts says looking back on that day, 'was that she didn't see herself as anything special. It was quite normal for her to join in even though the onlookers seeing her in callipers were amazed and impressed by seeing a child doing something there was no need for her to do. It was Tanni's special quality that she never recognized or used her disability as an excuse not to take a full part in everything.

In time Tanni came to accept the attention and curiosity of outsiders as a fact of her life.

'There were,' she says, 'one or two other occasions when I was asked to pick up a charity cheque from someone because I was the cute kid in a wheelchair for the photo. And there were people who used to literally pat me on the head or treat me as if I was a bit daft. But it didn't bother me too much because I would try and ignore them and put their attitude down to their own stupidity. It wasn't my problem it was theirs.'

Sulwen has a different perspective on such incidents looking less at the attitude behind such incidents and more at the motive. She tells of one day when the family went out for a Saturday evening meal. A man walked past them and stopped to look at Tanni. He was black, Sulwen recalls, and very ordinarily dressed.

He then pressed a pound note into her hand. 'I feel so humble, ever so humble,' he said. Tears were running down his face and by then Tanni and I were not in much better a state. He said please take it. I had never seen him before and have never seen him since.'

From the very start of her problems with walking, Tanni's disability was not allowed to dominate family life.

'I was brought up in an able-bodied environment and did not think of myself as having a disability because, at that age, it did not occur to me that I was any different. I never really had much contact with other disabled people.'

Tanni reflects that she and her sister Sian grew up in a caring family atmosphere being encouraged, loved and, if need be, corrected in a very normal way. Unlike some families where a disabled child dominates and distorts the home, this was not the case in the Grey household. Sian, who would have nothing to do with her little sister at school, had to share a bedroom with her at home until they were teenagers. Inevitably they argued, but they also ganged up with each other if a third party began to criticize either of them. Squabbles, when young, included who should sit with her back to the taps when they shared a bath and, when older, who should get up and switch the bedroom light off.

From the age of eight to thirteen Tanni went once a week for horse-riding lessons. It was the only activity which gave her any regular contact with other disabled people.

The Heath Cardiff Riding for Disabled group was started by Dinah Cadogan, a physiotherapy teacher at the University hospital of Wales. She was not a horsy person herself, admitting that all she knew about horses was that they 'bit at the front and kicked at the back', but she had the insight to appreciate that disabled young people would find riding a liberating activity.

'The experience for many children living in a wheelchair,' Dinah Cadogan observed, 'is that they're looked down upon in the physical sense. On a horse they are given height and that gives them a tremendous psychological boost. In nice weather they can ride through the lanes and across the fields and reach up and feel things such as a leaf. There is so much they can do on a horse that they miss out on in a wheelchair.'

Tanni joined the group in the September 1977 and was one of the first riders. There were half-a-dozen other children with helpers and the instructors at the Cardiff Equestrian Centre selected the ponies best suited for beginners.

'From the very beginning, we could see that Tanni had tremendous potential. She was a lovely bright child, with sparkling eyes and a ready smile who wanted to do things, and we knew that with the right kind of help and guidance she could go a very long way.'

Tanni became an adept rider and even progressed to jumps. She remembers, in particular, a pony called Silver. On at least three occasions she fell off, landing face down in the dirt and winding herself, but her pride was more wounded than her person. Not having the use of her legs Tanni held the reins with one hand, used the other to keep her balance, and controlled the horse with tickles of the whip.

'I trotted and cantered and enjoyed getting around so much faster than I could in my wheelchair.'

Sian also rode. She had lessons with another group at the same centre learning alongside Tanni but sometimes rode with

Tanni's class if there was a spare horse. She remembers falling off frequently and returning in a bruised and battered state.

'Sian was always given Paddy,' says Tanni. 'Paddy was like a cart horse and when she fell off it was a long way down to the ground.'

The riding group deliberately selected children who came from different schools and areas and did not know each other. This was so that they would have a chance of meeting new people. It was a new experience for Tanni in that, up until then, she had lived entirely in the able-bodied world, not separated from it as so many disabled children are. Consequently, as much as Tanni enjoyed the freedom and the challenge of horseriding, she felt that she had little in common with her fellow horse riders and often wondered why she was there with 'these people'.

Perhaps this attitude was coloured by the difference she noted between her own parents' treatment of her and the protective attitudes adopted by other parents towards their disabled children. On one occasion, when she was eleven, Tanni asked to be allowed to go away for a holiday break with the group to ride at Bridgend, some fifteen or twenty miles away. The plan was that the riders and their small team of helpers would be away from home, living in caravans and, as well as riding and pony trekking, would have the chance to go to a funfair and have a barbecue. Sulwen and Peter readily agreed.

In the same riding group Sulwen recalls there was a young disabled woman some years older than Tanni. When her mother heard that Sulwen was allowing Tanni to go away from home she was astonished.

'I'm not letting my daughter go' she said. 'She would miss her goodnight story and her kiss and cuddle.'

It was this remark that brought home to Sulwen and Peter that the mother's attitude was wrong. She was wrapping her child in emotional cotton wool and they were more determined than ever to avoid this kind of approach with Tanni. Sulwen is now outspoken about parents who take this over-protective approach to their disabled children. She describes it as a form of cruelty which prevents a disabled child from having any independence.

'Sometimes I think I must have been cruel to be kind,' Sulwen now says. 'If there was something that Tanni wanted and could reach, I just let her work out how to get it for herself. "I'm not your lackey" I used to say, "get it yourself".'

Peter and Sulwen never felt that they had a great deal in common with parents who, in their eyes, molly-coddled their disabled children. And they did not join the Spina Bifida and Hydrocephalus Association because they thought this would involve them in spending time discussing their child's problems with other people.

'A lot of parents want to discuss all the symptoms of their child's case.' Sulwen says. 'And before you know it you've convinced yourself your kid has got the same trouble. I didn't want to know about all that. Maybe I was a bit of an ostrich burying my head in the sand, but I didn't want to delve too deeply.'

'We were willing,' Peter emphasizes, 'to take Tanni anywhere so that she could do the things she wanted to do. But we were determined not do anything for her that she could do for herself.'

Peter and Sulwen have however maintained their interest in the Heath Cardiff Riding for Disabled group and Peter is still the secretary/treasurer. Tanni too, although she gave up riding as a hobby around the time she had a major operation on her spine, is willing to offer her help when she can. She is currently Vice-President of the South Wales region of Riding for Disabled, and visits events to hand out rosettes and cups and offer her encouragement to others.

As an outside observer, Dinah Cadogan is quite sure that Peter's, Sulwen's and Sian's attitude, had much to do with Tanni's successful approach to life.

'Unfortunately, there are some parents who moan "we've got a handicapped child and life is very hard on us" and they look at all the negative sides. But, from the beginning, Sulwen and Peter made up their minds that Tanni would be as active as she could possibly be.'

Lessons were learned quickly that way. When, for instance, Tanni was about eight or nine, her mother left her by herself in her wheelchair at a local shopping centre so that Tanni could do some shopping unaided.

'Mum insisted that I manage on my own. I remember trying to open the door of Boots the Chemist in my wheelchair and not being able to get my chair through because I couldn't push the door properly. I also remember people just walking past and looking down at me as I carried on struggling. Then a punk, with a freaky hair-do, shaved down both sides and shocking pink on the top, who had been hanging around opposite came along and started talking to me. He opened the door.'

Tanni also became aware of people staring at her and remembers thinking how stupid they were. Why did they have a problem with seeing someone in a wheelchair?

Today, along with thousands of other wheelchair-users, Tanni still gets 'weird looks' in public places.

'I am so used to people staring that I just ignore it. A short while ago, I was in London with my mother and she pointed out that people were looking at us as if I was odd. But I hadn't even noticed. At university too, my friends would notice people staring at me because of my wheelchair. But, to be honest, I seldom notice anymore and, if I do, I just stare back. What really bugs me more than anything else is if someone walks past pretending they're not looking at me and then sneaks a look out of the corner of their eye.'

This coy, embarrassed approach to disability is something that seems to creep up on able-bodied people towards adulthood. Children, Tanni recalls from her childhood days, are more accepting and direct. And as Dinah Cadogan has observed, not only through her contact with disabled young people horseriding but also through her forty-five years experience as a leader in the Brownie organization, 'It's the adults who go "aah" or "poor little thing" when they see a child in a wheelchair. The children, provided you have talked to them sensibly about disability beforehand, don't take any notice'.

Already a Brownie at Brichgrove school, Tanni joined Dinah Cadogan's Pack when Dinah suggested that she might be interested in going away with the group on a holiday. Dinah appreciated the problems that Peter and Sulwen might face in taking Tanni to an ordinary holiday place. Too often parents of disabled children are subjected to stares and criticisms and unwanted sympathy.

'Tanni couldn't come away with us on holiday unless she was a member of the pack,' Dinah recalled, 'but that problem was resolved when she joined up for a few months before we went away.She fitted in exactly the same as the other Brownies. She was one of two Brownies in the pack in a wheelchair. I was very determined that she wasn't going to be the only wheelchair user because I didn't want her to have special treatment!'

Tanni's first Brownie Pack Holiday was not too far from home, in Swansea. All the Brownies had to take turns with the chores and if washing-up was on the rota Tanni too had her bowl of water.

Even when the other Brownies were skipping, the two girls in their wheelchairs found a way of joining in. Tanni found she could push her body in the chair down a slope and take two hands off the wheels and swing the rope over.

She also went on the swings, although she did need a cushion on the seat and her legs needed to be tied up to prevent them scuffing on the ground. There was also a roundabout, and some of the Brownies found a way of pushing the wheelchairs on to this through a gap.

'Before Tanni and Mair joined the Pack in their wheelchairs, we talked to the girls and explained that, although the two new Brownies were unable to walk, they could do many things and would be able to join in most activities. The other Pack members were marvellous. They understood that they had to be sensible and took things at a reasonable pace. A number of those children eventually became nurses, doctors and physiotherapists. Who knows, perhaps that came about through the influence of what they learnt at that age!'

The fact that Tanni influenced her fellow Brownies in this way was perhaps an unexpected side-effect of her involvement. The more direct and observable impact at the time was Tanni's enthusiasm. In almost everything she was game to try anything and able to hold her own. She became a Brownie sixer, helping the adults to look after the younger ones in the Pack.

'This,' Dinah remembers, 'rubbed off on the other children, who then thought if Tanni could do it, so could they. Her presence in the Pack also helped the other children to become more considerate. They realized, for example, that they should not leave things on the floor because Tanni's and Mair's wheels would get caught up in the object.'

It was in the Brownies that Tanni developed her unique method of bouncing down steps. Getting to the place where the Brownies met involved negotiating a couple of steps with no ramp to help. A little ramp was made and often used, but it could not be left in place all the time. When she first joined the Brownies, Tanni was still using the callipers as well as the wheelchair and was still at the stage of learning how to make the most of her new wheels. Dinah, as a physiotherapy teacher, recalls offering Tanni advice on how best to move in and out of her wheelchair from the floor or a chair so that she could heave her own way up the steps if the ramp was not in position.

'Tanni was unusual,' Dinah recalls, 'in that she was not embarrassed. She needed to develop the skills of independence because, although while she was little her parents and others could carry her up and downstairs, when she was heavier it would be a considerable struggle.'

Tanni became so adept at such independent mobility manoeuvres and was so unfazed by having to perform them in front of other people that Dinah asked her, when she was a teenager, to help her with an adult training programme for the Girl Guides in Wales. The point of the programme was to enable adults to understand more about disability.

'She came and spoke to the group and showed them how she moved and how she could get herself up and down stairs completely independently. She explained her point of view to the adults and allowed them to carry her in a special seat which had been designed for use in situations where it was not possible to take a wheelchair. She was a very willing guinea pig and was quite willing to tell people where things were going right and where they were doing things wrong. It was very unusual in a teenager, but Tanni was extremely outgoing and very helpful.'

Tanni was also uninhibited in the sense that she would talk openly about her disability. She would explain to the other children that she had little feeling in her legs and that if they bumped her she might damage them. She would also, if she needed it, ask for help in putting on her callipers. But at the same time she was not pushy or aggressively outgoing. She had just the right blend of openness and reserve and simply got on with life as she knew it with no self-pity or introspection.

'She would not shout about what she could do,' Dinah remembers. 'She would just quietly get on and do it. When it was Tanni's turn she would do what she had to with no special fuss or boasting. I think this was a very important part of her development because if she had made a nuisance of herself I do not think people would have responded in the same way. She had a natural reserve, was quite shy in some ways, and was a very kind and very willing child.'

One moment during Tanni's childhood, which Sulwen vividly recalls was when she turned to Tanni and asked: 'What do you think about having spina bifida?'.

It was typical of Tanni, even as a child, not to spend time on abstract questions, but to tackle the practical implications of the condition.

'I can't do anything about it, can I?' Tanni replied. 'I've got to get on with it.'

Nobody had said anything to Tanni, but that was her attitude. She just had to get on with life as it was.

Sulwen adds however that she and Peter were very fortunate that Tanni was the type of girl she was – determined right from the word go.

Looking back on the early years Tanni speculates that her parents' attitude towards her may well, in part, have been shaped by Sian's earlier illness.

'Shortly after I was born,' she says, 'Sian needed a lot of care. And when at first sight there did not appear to be a lot wrong with me, Sian's health was my parents' first priority and they didn't completely panic and try and over-protect me.'

There was a time, Peter recalls, when both girls were 'a mess'

'One week Tanni would be all right and we would worry about Sian. If we were chasing to see Sian in hospital Tanni just had to bustle along.'

It would certainly be inaccurate to give the impression that Tanni's disability did not in any way affect the family. Sian's condition was treatable, Tanni needed to be taken at regular intervals to see clinic specialists who, in due course, advised medical intervention.

As a young child Tanni had to become used to these periodic check-ups when her back, kidneys and limb function were measured and monitored. She remembers the boredom of waiting rooms and of how her mother and father had to try to keep her amused surrounded by hosts of other ratty children awaiting their turn.

Children with spina bifida can develop a curvature of the spine which both diminishes their height and affects the ability for certain organs to function properly. The defect itself can be marginally improved by surgery, but additional problems can arise as the body's bone and muscular structure grows throughout childhood.

'Although neurologically the condition is basically static,' Dr Weisl explains, 'skeletally the children tend to deteriorate because they are growing. And as long as they are growing they can be subject to an imbalance of muscle pulls. The way in which nerve roots come out of the spinal cord and go to different muscles is a fairly complex arrangement. Specific weaknesses can develop for the different levels of neurological damage and the weaknesses are not symmetrical. Some children, for instance, can bend their hips but are unable to stand because they do not have any muscles in their buttocks to hold them up. They might be able to bend their knees but not straighten them because different nerves are affected.'

When Tanni was seven, Sulwen and Peter were advised that she needed an operation. She had not been operated on at birth because the lump on her back, which she referred to as her 'bump', was covered in skin and not exposed. By the age of seven, however, it was felt that the surgeon needed to find out more about the precise nature of her spina bifida. The 'bump' was not causing Tanni any great problems except that if she banged it she had a sensation similar to that from the funny bone, a sharp jolt followed by a tingle.

On one such occasion, two or three years earlier, when Tanni had knocked her bump as she was coming down the stairs, she displayed a somewhat different attitude to her condition than the one she later relayed so philosophically to her mother. She had learned some swear words from her grandfather and was seen sitting at the bottom of the stairs muttering: 'My bloody bump, you stupid bugger!' or words to that effect!

In hospital, having opened up and carefully examined the 'bloody bump', the surgeon, Mr Robert Weekes, cut away the fatty tissue and tucked the exposed spinal cord back into the spinal column. He generally tidied up the area and made some initial preparations for an operation that Tanni would need some years later when her back had grown and developed more.

A lump of Tanni's type consists of fat and nerves, and often the nerve roots are mixed up with the fat making it a difficult and painstaking procedure.

What had been planned as an hour-long exploratory procedure actually took four hours. Afterwards Tanni's back was noticeably flatter and the jolts and tingles Tanni experienced when she knocked her back disappeared. It was the first of three major operations on her back which Tanni was to have.

There was no single moment during Tanni's childhood when she realized that she had totally lost her ability to walk. It was a gradual process beginning with the falling-down stage when she started school through to the end of her years at Birchgrove when she needed to use her wheelchair almost full time. Even then she was not totally reliant on her chair, for she developed other ways of getting around on the floor and her strong arm and shoulder muscles gave her an added mobility around the house.

'As my body grew it squashed the spinal cord which increased the paralysis and so, over a fairly long period, I gradually lost the use of my legs. It wasn't that I woke up one day and couldn't walk. It wasn't like breaking my back and finding out overnight that I had to get used to a new life. I had a lot of time to get accustomed to the changes. I can still vaguely remember what it was like to walk, although I do not remember exactly what it was like to lose the use of my legs. I certainly don't remember being worried about it.

'Today the loss of muscular power and sensation starts from my waist down, but it kind of zigzags around my body and it's not as if it's one definite line. It brings problems with my bladder. I have to use a catheter. When I was young I was continent, but as the paralysis set in I experienced more and more problems throughout junior school.

'Now I just accept that there's absolutely nothing I can do to change my condition. Having to catheterize, to pass a special tube through into the bladder to empty it, is a nuisance. I know if I had three wishes, changing that would be my first. Being able to walk again would not be one of them because being in a wheelchair has given me a lot of positive things in life. But there is no point in thinking that I will ever get that wish. I tend to be like that. I don't believe there's going to be a magical cure. I don't think that one day I'm suddenly going to be different. What is the point in wishing my life away, thinking if only I could do this or that? I just can't. So, I might as well get on with it.'

This philosophy had been developed by – and instilled in – Tanni throughout her formative years. Despite life having dealt her certain disadvantages, she never felt that she was any different from her friends. She was Tanni, with a life to lead, experiences to grasp, much to learn and with numerous opportunities ahead. Why should her life be significantly different from that of her sister or her schoolmates? She assumed she would continue from primary school to secondary school in their company and it came as quite a shock to her and her parents when the South Glamorgan Education Authority took a different view. It was suggested that Tanni needed to be taken out of mainstream education and sent to a special school for a year with other disabled children from the county, in order to be assessed.

Tanni and her best friend Sue Roberts would have to go their own ways and Sue vividly remembers her disappointment:

'I was gutted,' she says.

CHAPTER TWO

Sports mad

*'I find it incredible that if you can walk,
nobody thinks you need a special education,
but if you're in a wheelchair they do.'*

WHEN THE TIME came for Tanni to progress from primary to
secondary school her sister was already well established at
Llanishen, the local comprehensive. Naturally it was assumed by
Sulwen and Peter that Tanni would follow in her footsteps.

They sought a preliminary meeting with the headmaster who,
without even meeting Tanni, decided that he could not accept a
pupil who used a wheelchair. The school, he said, did not have
access facilities, the site was unsuitable, and nothing that Tanni's
parents could say would change his mind. Looking back Sian is
quite sure that, with a few modifications, the school would have
had no difficulty in taking her sister. Nevertheless the headmaster was adamant in his refusal.

Neither Peter nor Sulwen are people to be cowed by those in
authority. Peter decided to research Tanni's rights and learned
from the relevant papers and acts of parliament that it is a local
authority's responsibility to educate all children according to
their capabilities, even if facilities are not immediately available
within the county.

So began a correspondence between the South Glamorgan
Education Authority and Tanni's parents. Peter and Sulwen were
determined that the education of their transparently intelligent
daughter should not be held back simply because she used a
wheelchair. They were both great believers in the value of

education and were firmly of the opinion that, whatever might happen to Tanni in later life, her education and qualifications would be all important.

In due course the Education Authority decided to make its own assessment of Tanni's capabilities and suggested that, first, she should go to Erw'r Delyn, a special school for disabled children, for her abilities to be monitored. Sulwen and Peter were quite sure that if this was to happen a whole year of education would be lost and Tanni would lose all the impetus that she had gained from Birchgrove. They also felt that if Tanni was sent to a special school she would not be stretched and would perhaps learn how to play on her disability to get sympathy and an easier life. They were even prepared to allow Tanni to be taken away from Wales to a boarding school as long as it meant that her normal education would not be impaired.

Tanni's parents pointed out that all the assessments could be made while Tanni was still at primary school and that the teachers there would know all about her academic abilities. The Education Authority then agreed to send someone to Birchgrove to judge Tanni's capabilities in situ. She was also sent to see a psychologist who Peter now describes as a 'nutter'.

'I find it incredible,' Tanni says looking back, 'that because I was in a wheelchair I had to go through all these assessments. The Education Authority's attitude seemed to be that you could be as thick as two short planks but as long as you could walk through the gates of the school you had a right to go there. It was an incredible presumption that if you can walk you don't need special education, but if you're in a wheelchair you do. Later, throughout school, I met many kids who could have benefited from special education, but because they could walk and didn't appear to have a disability they didn't get it.'

Tanni has a number of memories of her parents' battle with South Glamorgan Education Authority.

'When I came back from school, Mum was always asking me if anybody unusual had been to see me. One day a man did come. I remember him standing in the door of the classroom looking

47

at me. After a while he came up, said a few words, and asked me what I was doing. And that was how he carried out his official assessment of me. I remember being amazed at how clever he was, that he could assess my suitability for mainstream education by doing little more than looking at me from the doorway.

'Then, later, I had to go for an interview and a man kept asking me some really dim questions, "How many days in a year?", "In which direction does the sun rise?", "How do you make the colour brown?". I remember sitting there thinking "What is this man on about?".

'All this hassle seemed really crazy at the time. I was just Tanni and happened to use a wheelchair. It had never occurred to me that there would be such a problem. And it changed me. I began to think differently. It brought home to me that I was thought of as different.'

Later Tanni was to meet and race against Tracey Lewis who, although six years older, recalls a very similar experience. It was clearly not just in South Wales that education authorities had problems with allowing disabled children full access to main-stream secondary education.

After going to a mainstream junior school Tracey had to go away as a boarder at the age of eleven to a special school in Hampshire where she stayed until she was seventeen. Tracey, who also has spina bifida, described the school as 'not too bad' and the best in the country at the time. She still finds it strange, however, that simply because of her mobility problems her education had to take place away from home and the friends that she had made.

Eventually it was suggested that Tanni should consider a school, St Cyres, some ten miles away, which was next door to Erw'r Delyn the special school. While she was at St Cyres, receiving a mainstream education, she would then also have the tailor-made facilities of Erw'r Delyn on the doorstep should she need them.

In a mood for a fight, and not sure at that time whether they were being fobbed off with second best, Peter and Sulwen went to see the headmaster of St Cyres. They were not expecting South Glamorgan to agree to an arrangement which would meet all their requirements and, by that time, were even considering home education for Tanni.

However, on arrival at the school, they found that not only was it, for its time, well geared up to dealing with wheelchairs but the headmaster was welcoming and said that he would be delighted to have Tanni.

The choice of schools settled, Tanni now had to be taken ten miles by taxi every morning to school. Travel aside, going from the friendly Birchgrove to a secondary school with well over a thousand pupils was a culture shock. Neither her sister nor her close schoolfriends were with her. She was a new girl, in a new environment and was conspicuous because of her wheelchair. She was one of a group of thirty other wheelchair-users who often had to wait around to be carried up and down stairs by helpers.

There were five or six people, known as the wheelchair-lifters, who in break times and between lessons had to take all the children in wheelchairs up and down stairs. Tanni might have been able to manage the stairs herself but it was a matter of time and a question of safety. With children running around the building, needing to get from one classroom to the next, Tanni would have run the risk of being trodden on or being the cause of someone else's downfall. Even with the lifters working at speed Tanni would often be late for classes and the teachers, unfairly, would be annoyed with her.

There was, in fact, often absolute chaos between classes and breaks as the lifters tried to move the wheelchairs up and down the stairs. It was certainly an unsatisfactory arrangement with the fear at the back of every teacher's mind that in the event of a fire it could well be that the disabled pupils would be the last out of the building. A fact which was implicitly, if not explicitly, accepted by the staff.

'For the first couple of years I had to go across to Erw'r Delyn for lunch,' Tanni said, 'because those of us with disabilities were not allowed to have lunch in the main school. There were some who needed special medical treatment at lunchtime so there probably was a need for them to go somewhere else, but I didn't see why I should.'

Tanni was the only wheelchair-user in her form and, right from the start, the friends that she made were largely able-bodied. Fellow new girl Jo Dutch and Tanni became firm friends from the very early days. Jo had had little contact with disabled children before and, although she was very aware of the wheelchair at the start, it was not long before Tanni's personality and independence became much more important than the wheelchair.

Tanni's form teacher, Mrs Gill Thomas, speaking just a few days before she died in the autumn of 1995, told of her vivid recollection of Tanni on her first day.

'The children all stood in the hall, a long list of names was read out and one by one they come forward. It was the first time I had had a wheelchair pupil in my class and my first reaction was "Oh my God, what am I going to do?". I could see problems ahead because my form was in a room in an annexe. I also noticed how small Tanni was, minute, with this absolutely angelic face. She was very shy to start off with but her personality soon emerged. She was a little monkey with a twinkle in her eye!

'She had callipers and her mother used to say to me that I should persuade her to walk. She would occasionally but reluctantly. She also had crutches but tended to hold these outwards, not under the armpits. As a result it was chaos in the corridors because people would either trip over her or trip her up. Not surprisingly, she found it easier to use the chair and no amount of nagging would get her to use her callipers.'

As form teacher it was Mrs Thomas's job to take the register in the morning and Tanni's name also gave her problems. Was she to be known officially as Tanni or Carys? The two names together would not fit into the space provided in the register! In the event, everyone agreed that Tanni was Tanni.

At her new school Tanni quickly made new friends and, just as she had been at the junior school, was frequently at the centre of the loudest group in the playground. Mrs Thomas certainly never noticed any teasing or bullying. She did remember one disabled girl receiving some unpleasant treatment but that, she believed, was largely because of the girl's less-than-pleasant personality. Friends, however, rallied round Tanni 'like bees round a honeypot', to borrow a phrase of Mrs Thomas. 'She gathered in friends very easily, boys as well as girls.'

'She was,' Jo Dutch recalls, 'always a very strong person with strong ideas, and people had a fine regard for her.'

In class, few allowances were made for Tanni but sometimes adaptations had to be made. One day Mrs Thomas noticed Tanni in a cookery class balanced precariously on the arm of her chair at the cooker. So a special low surface was made from which Tanni could work and, with the addition of a two-ring burner, she was able to do all the practical work that was required.

Tanni's great advantage was that she was agile and could always devise ways of humping herself on to a stool or a chair. She was also very determined that anything she could do for herself she would. Sometimes Tanni and Mrs Thomas had to use their imagination to overcome problems. In Tanni's first year, for example, her class was due to plan and lead a school assembly. It was Christmas week, but how could Tanni, in her wheelchair, fit into a nativity scene? In the end the class arranged a tableau with Tanni wrapped in a blue sheet holding a plastic doll. With her innocent face she made an ideal Virgin Mary.

'For a lot of the handicapped children,' Mrs Thomas said, recalling her experience at St Cyres, 'teachers had to fetch and carry all the time, but Tanni was very independent. This was wonderful because while you were seeing to two or three handicapped children all the time, the rest of the class would go to pot. With Tanni the only thing that caused a problem was getting in and out of the storeroom. It was like Piccadilly Circus there because if Tanni was trying to go in she would block the storeroom for everybody else and could not then always reach the equipment high up on the shelves. These problems were resolved when we were given a housecraft assistant who could help Tanni and others to get things from the storeroom. I also remember that when Tanni was taking her 'O' levels, we needed special permission for the housecraft assistant to act as Tanni's fetcher to get what she needed from the high shelves.'

Mrs Thomas also recalls that the headmaster of Erw'r Delyn was a traditionalist – and a very strict man. He was also enlightened in that he was determined that the disabled children in his care should be described as normal and treated as normal.

'In the beginning,' she added, 'I felt I *had* to be nice to all of them, but some were awfully naughty and rude.'

Over the years at the school Mrs Thomas noticed that Tanni's attitude to her disability differed from that of many of the other children in wheelchairs.

'Some of the children seemed to have a chip on their shoulder, but not Tanni – not at all. I think this was probably due to her family background, her parents pushed her on.'

Through her secondary school years Tanni was gaining a wider perspective on her disability and what it means to be a disabled person in late twentieth-century Britain. She also gained a valuable and broadening experience in 1981 when she was taken with a party of disabled adults and children to Lourdes, the world-famous French site of pilgrimage.

Although she had gained a certificate of merit from the National Christian Education Council for a scripture exam the year before, Tanni was not, and is not, a very religious person. The invitation to Lourdes, however, was accepted because it both intrigued her and gave her an excuse to see more of the world.

'But she doesn't like cricket,' Sulwen initially replied before realizing that the suggested trip was to France and not St John's Wood!

Lourdes is renowned as a place of miraculous healing. How many of the discarded crutches on display are real evidence that their former owners can now walk unaided is open to question but many people who visit the shrine acknowledge that, amidst the crowds and the carnival atmosphere, many people do find an inner healing. This does not usually take the form of a physical cure but it does give a vital boost to hope and self-esteem.

'We went by train and had such good fun.' Tanni said. 'There were so many groups that my group from Cardiff had to wear yellow and brown bobble hats so that we could be identified in the crowd. The priest with us asked me if I would like to go into the water. The weather was cold, so I asked him if the water was freezing as well. "Bloody freezing," he said, "so I'll sprinkle some water over you – it'll have the same effect."'

Being clubbed together with a crowd of disabled people was not what Tanni usually enjoyed, but after her first year at secondary school, she was getting used to being with other people with disabilities and was less worried by it than she would have been a couple of years earlier.

'Before we went we were told about Lourdes and the miracles, but I just saw the trip as a jaunt away. For as long as I can remember I have always known there will never be a cure for me, so I had no ambitions to come away from the shrine walking. By the age of eleven, I had figured out that things were not going to change, life was going to be lived in a wheelchair, so I treated Lourdes simply as an experience and a holiday.

'I learned a lot about other disabilities, however, and I was fascinated by the atmosphere of the place, the elaborate services with all the incense, as well as the tacky souvenirs – plastic Mary-shaped bottles for holy water and the like.'

Tanni was however still unwilling to be stereotyped at school or, as she sometimes viewed it, ghettoised with the other disabled pupils.

'It was the rule that the disabled pupils went to Erw'r Delyn for PE lessons and lunchtimes. I resented that and did everything I could not to have to go to the special school. I really did not see why I should go there when I wanted to be with my friends in the mainstream school.'

There were also some minor but, to Tanni and her parents, unnecessary features of life at Erw'r Delyn. Sulwen, for example, spotted one such insensitivity that she did not like at all. Many of the children, like Tanni, needed to catheterize and one of the teachers would shout reminders along the corridor. 'That is not the sort of thing you shout out loud to a fourteen year old girl.' Sulwen said. 'At that age they are naturally very self-conscious about such personal things.'

Jo Dutch recalls there being quite a lot of contact between the children from Erw'r Delyn and those from St Cyres. 'But,' she added, 'Tanni stayed with us all of the time for lessons.'

Within two or three years Tanni had settled down and had discovered both how to survive and manipulate the system. She avoided going across to Erw'r Delyn for meals by volunteering to do extra lessons around lunchtime at St Cyres. This, of course, gave her little time to go for her midday meal in the other place!

Having got Tanni accepted by St Cyres was not the end of her parents' tussle with the Education Authority. Once again, at the age of thirteen, Tanni had to see a psychologist so that he could determine whether she was capable of staying on at mainstream school.

Then, at the age of fifteen, when she had done her 'O' levels, she had to be assessed for a third time. Having proven that she could cope, and cope well, with mainstream education, she was only too conscious that the attitude of the educationalists showed little awareness of this.

'They offered,' Tanni said, 'to get me "a nice place in a little secretarial college". I stated bluntly that I did not want to be a secretary. Their response was an eye-opener. "But you're in a wheelchair."'

This approach was like a red rag to a bull. Tanni was now a confident teenager with opinions and a determination not to be pigeon-holed into the kind of job deemed suitable by society for a disabled person. 'What's that got to do with anything?' she demanded.

The idea that she might one day become a professional athlete had not yet crossed her mind. Indeed at that time there were no full-time Paralympians and the notion that there might be some time in the future was inconceivable. Tanni's appetite for sport however had been whetted. Whatever her thoughts about having to attend Erw'r Delyn for lunch and certain other activities, the school did give Tanni the opportunity to try out a range of sports. To horse riding she added archery, basketball, swimming and tennis.

Mrs Thomas described one occasion when Tanni was at a school party in the pool at the Swansea leisure centre. She slid down a slope into the water on her haunches and, once in the water, gained a freedom of movement that she could never have achieved on dry land.

'Learning to swim was very exciting,' Tanni recalls. 'I am still not very good– my legs just float in the water but it's something I enjoy very much.'

At the age of thirteen however, Tanni's enthusiasm for sport had to be curtailed when strain on her damaged spine began to cause concern. Up until then, apart from a tendency to pick up regular urinary tract infections, she had remained healthy. Now, as she entered her teens, Tanni began to experience a lot of pain as her spine curved and began to pull the ribs round and distort the shape of her body. She soon found herself in hospital requiring major surgery on her back.

'It is a fairly common problem with spina bifida,' she said, 'and it happened to me fairly quickly from about the age of eleven. I used to have check-ups every six months and, when I went for my usual check-up in December, I was told I would have to go into hospital very soon for an operation.'

Sulwen remembers how anxious she and Tanni always felt before each of the six-monthly visits. They knew that sooner or later the operation would be necessary and that in due course they would be told to prepare for a difficult stay in hospital.

'By the time the consultant suggested operating,' Sulwen said, 'Tanni was in considerable pain. She would come home from school and would need to lie on her bed to ease her aching back.'

The consultant, David Jenkins, discussed each stage of his proposed treatment with Tanni in detail. Although Sulwen and Peter were there listening, it was Tanni he addressed and Tanni, at the age of thirteen, who was expected to understand and take her share of the responsibility for decisions.

'I was actually given a choice. Did I want the operation? And I remember saying "Well, do I need it?". When they said "yes", I said, "Okay, fine".

'I had a metal rod put in my spine. If this had not been done I might have become more paralysed. The operation was painful. I had to stay in hospital for three weeks and afterwards I had to be in a plastercast jacket from my neck to my waist for six months. This became a bit grotty with time because the jacket smelt.'

When Tanni was in hospital, in January 1983, Sian visited her regularly after school. Sian remembers 'turning up one day to find Tanni sporting a yellow bow, tied around her neck, from a well-wisher's bouquet of flowers!'

Mrs Thomas recalled visiting Tanni in the hospital to take her homework and to keep her up to date with the lessons being set for her class.

Sometimes too, Tanni would find her father there. He would come in early to give her breakfast. Officially visiting hours had not started but as he worked for the National Health Service, he found he could take opportunities for unofficial visits. He joked to Mrs Thomas that he would come in with his clipboard and measuring tape and, if challenged, would start measuring the corridor.

In the end, just before her fourteenth birthday in July 1983, the neck-to-waist plaster jacket was removed. During the time she had been encased, a bedroom had been made for her downstairs at home and she moved from sharing with Sian to having her own space in the girls' old playroom.

She had become quite used to getting around with the plaster jacket on but it was not a comfortable experience. While she waited for her spine to heal, she buoyed herself up with the thought that, once the ordeal was over, she would be able to return to playing sport.

When the moment came however for the plaster to be cut away, she was dismayed to find that the muscles in her back and neck were exceedingly weak. When she sat up for the first time her head just flopped over to one side. She was taken to be X-rayed and was asked if she could stand if two people held her. But she could not even hold her head straight, let alone stand with assistance.

'To get the X-ray they insisted I had to hold my head up. I remember it just wobbling back and forth. I literally had to hold on to my head to keep it up and my mother and sister thought this was hysterically funny. It took a week of struggling before I was able to sit up but in time the strength in my muscles returned.'

Once Tanni was fit again she was able to resume her sporting activities. The more she did, the more she practised, the more her muscles returned to normal – and then strengthened even further. Looking back Tanni believes that the additional strength and fitness she gained from her athletics training not only enabled her to stay free of the infections which had plagued her when young, but also gave extra support to her spine.

'One of the reasons my spine was weak,' she said, 'is that the muscles in my back were weak. This was partly due to the type of wheelchair I was sitting in at the time. It was the accepted thing then that all kids in chairs should have them designed with high backs. Also I had very little physiotherapy and, although I did PE at school, I did not do a great deal of exercise outside. With hindsight, it would have been better to have done a lot more sport at school to strengthen the muscles I had. When I started losing the use of my legs I do not recall being given any extra physio to preserve what use I had. Since starting to compete I have become a lot fitter.'

For all her determination to remain in mainstream education and her reluctance to become too closely identified with Erw'r Delyn school, it was there, the year before her operation, that Tanni had her first experience of wheelchair racing. In her ordinary National Health wheelchair, encouraged by Phil Helmore the PE teacher, she took part in the Erw'r Delyn Sports Day. It was the first time she had taken part in a disability sport.

'I really enjoyed it. I had done a lot of sports where I competed against able-bodied people, but it was good to be able to compete against others the same as me and not be beaten hands down – indeed, to be able to do quite well.'

Sulwen recalls Tanni announcing, on return from school one day, that the next day she was going to enter some races. Sulwen thought little more of this until Tanni arrived home clutching a pile of cups and shields. She had won them, she said, for a whole range of events including the 60-metres dash and the slalom. She had received the award for top all-round performance. On further questioning, Sulwen gathered that Tanni had not just been taking part in some gentle local races but an inter-school match.

It was becoming obvious that Tanni had a natural talent. She had a strength in her arms and shoulders, which combined with stamina, a natural rhythm, and an innate determination, enabled her to succeed and later to excel. Even in the days when she used heavy chariot-like wheelchairs, she had an exceptional agility which enabled her to manoeuvre, accelerate and brake. This, of course, gave her a great advantage in the slalom. As for her competitiveness, that came out not only on the track but in every other sport. As a junior basketball player, her competitive instinct was such that she was better known as an aggressive player rather than as a high scorer!

Her tendency to foul other players and even fight on court, Tanni now admits, was nothing short of obnoxious. Size was no deterrent to her and she would not flinch from fights with even the largest players. She did not like losing the ball to the other side. She played in defence and admits that, although she was not very good at the game, she never lacked courage.

Temperamentally, Tanni is not a good team player and is better suited to the pursuit of individual excellence. Her sister says, with the candour only a sister is allowed, that Tanni does not do anything as a team!

Wheelchair racing however did not immediately become her chief interest, even though throughout her secondary school years it became increasingly important. It was something she had to do apart from her main friends at St Cyres and Jo Dutch remembers how suddenly Tanni's success came. From merely being involved in general sport at Erw'r Delyn, she was suddenly racing competitively and travelling the country to do so.

In 1981 when a Welsh team was selected for the British Sports Association Junior National Games at Stoke Mandeville, Tanni was one of twelve Erw'r Delyn pupils chosen to be in the fifteen-strong Welsh team.

As a member of a national team for the first time Tanni took Gold in the girls' junior slalom and Silver in the 100-metres wheelchair dash. Altogether, the Welsh team took nine Golds and four Silvers.

Except for the year when Tanni spent six months in plaster, competing as a junior in both local and national events became a regular feature in her life. She also represented Wales as a member of the basketball team.

'I did not have my own racing chair then – I borrowed the school's. There were not any opportunities to have a chair of my own with which to train; and I didn't even know this was possible. It was not until I was seventeen and leaving the junior division that I thought, if I want to continue competing after I leave school, I should look ahead and get my own chair.'

Many young people who take part in sport at school are only too glad to give it up when they leave. Of those who show promise, only a minority continue taking part once it is no longer compulsory, and only a minority seek to join a club. Tanni however had a particular incentive to continue with wheelchair racing. She had tasted success and by 1985, her achievements and personality had been rewarded with her first major award. She became the Junior Personality of the Year at the Rotary Welsh Sports Team Championship.

Among the wins on the track, which acted as a particular spur, was her 1984 performance at Stoke Mandeville when she won the 100 metres by a considerable margin and, just after crossing the finishing line, heard that she had set a new British junior record.

Away from the sports field, Tanni progressed through secondary schooling towards her 'O' levels and was one of her year's academic achievers. She gained nine passes, including two As and five Bs, and set her mind on going to university. The concerns expressed by the educationalists throughout the years, that her disability might impair her academic work, proved to be nonsense.

She also went through her 'David Bowie stage', crossing swords, as all teenagers do, with her mother about the clothes she should buy. Today, sister Sian still maintains that Tanni has no colour sense when it comes to choosing her wardrobe and that she acts as her 'consultant'.

Despite her alleged lack of colour sense, Tanni frequently experiments with dyeing her hair. It has been bleached, pink and ginger. Even at the age of six she persuaded her mother to let her try a wash-out temporary hair-colour to give her a different look. It turned out pink!

As they grew up, Tanni and her friends got up to more than their fair share of mischief.

'One thing we used to do,' says Jo Dutch, 'and it probably sounds really juvenile now, is go into the town with Tanni pushing herself in the wheelchair. We would then stop, so that she could get out and sit on a bench, then she would tell me to get into her chair and go up and down the street. Having done that and attracted people's attention, I would then get out of the chair and we would watch people's expressions as I started walking. They were totally shocked and that of course was the reason for doing it. We thought it was very funny!'

Jo also recalls an evening out that took place when they were fourteen or fifteen. They both heard that, to quote Jo, 'in this dive of a club' in Cardiff young women would be admitted for half price if they dressed up in a St Trinians' theme fancy dress. Tanni and Jo donned the right gear and, feeling idiotic, went into town. On arrival at the club they found fewer than half a dozen people dressed up and, feeling somewhat stupid, decided to leave after only half an hour and go to a Wimpy bar instead.

'We would also go to sixth-form parties,' she recalls, 'where there would be the obligatory under-age drinking and to a club called the 'Marconi' in Penarth. Although it wasn't easy for Tanni to get in to the Marconi because there were so many steps, we would carry her up and down. Tanni would then get on to the dance floor in her chair. Brilliant! You would think everyone would have stopped and stared at her, but they didn't. With everybody twirling round and joining in, it didn't seem to bother anybody at all, which was good.'

Their expeditions into town on Saturdays soon made Jo realize how badly designed many shops were for wheelchairs. The access was poor and the shop doors too heavy to push open. Also in clothes shops, the racks of clothes were invariably placed too close to each other for someone in a wheelchair to rummage through.

'Overall things have changed for the better, but twelve years ago it was not good.'

On one occasion Tanni went into Cardiff with another friend who used a wheelchair. At Marks and Spencer, as the friend pushed her wheelchair against the door to open it, she cracked the glass from top to bottom.

Occasionally too, Tanni and her friends would encounter the 'Does he take sugar?' syndrome. People in shops would ignore Tanni in the chair and address the able-bodied friend. Most of the time Tanni would laugh this off but she admits she was conscious of it happening and bothered by it. She was especially annoyed on the occasions when she paid for something in a shop and the assistant then handed the change over to the friend standing with her. Often that friend was Jo Dutch who felt as angry as Tanni, but she cannot remember a single occasion, however sorely tempted they were, when they let their feelings be known.

Since then to the present day, Tanni has built up a dossier of shops which she now boycotts. Even if the front door is accessible, a shop which inside provides awkward steps and hurdles for a wheelchair-user, is bypassed. She takes the attitude:

'Stuff them – if they're not going to make provision for me, I'm not going to buy from them.'

At the age of seventeen Tanni took and passed her driving test and the freedom that this gave enabled her to lead an even more independent life as a sixth-former than many of her friends.

'I used to wear a lot of black in the sixth form – it was fashionable back then – and I dossed around in jeans and T-shirts. There were parties to go to and, until I was driving myself, Mum was absolutely great in driving me to and fro and picking me up at all hours of the day and night. To be honest, I think she was happier knowing she could pick me up at a certain time in the morning rather than leaving me to my own devices!

'There was a pub with a really grotty disco upstairs which everyone from school went to. I didn't do much dancing, but I would go along to be with my friends and to talk the usual sort of teenage nonsense.'

'But, in general,' Tanni adds, 'we were a fairly studious lot, not exactly swots, but most of us wanted to go on to further education.'

Tanni's continued interest in sport throughout the sixth form meant that she maintained her contacts with Erw'r Delyn. That aside, she remained a fully-integrated member of St Cyres and enjoyed the privileges of being a sixth-former. The sixth-form common room however was on the second floor which meant she could not take full advantage of everything that was available to those who had worked their way up to be senior pupils in the school. Getting up to the common room was hard work, although coming down was easier when friends offered to carry her chair.

As sixth formers, 'A' levels had to take priority over parties, discos and shopping. Tanni took four of the Advanced exams in English, General Studies, History and Computer Studies. She took an additional 'S' level in computer studies: 'when we had our first Apple at school, I was amazed by what it could do.'

When it came to applying for a university place Tanni opted for five – East Anglia, Reading, Leeds, Loughborough and

Swansea. She received offers from all of them. In the end, she decided against East Anglia because if she developed a medical problem it would be too far away to get home. 'Sometimes in my life I have to be realistic. The idea of being ill as far away from home as East Anglia did not appeal. To this day, if I'm ill I like to go home and be looked after.'

She then rejected Swansea because it was too close to home and she wanted to lead an independent life. The compromise was Loughborough – not that it was just a compromise. Tanni was keen to go there for its sports facilities. The campus was wheelchair-friendly and the university authorities were willing to adapt accommodation to her needs. Initially she had planned to study history, but when her chosen course closed down just before she took her 'A' levels she transferred to politics.

Loughborough University of Technology is world famous as a centre of sporting excellence. And if Tanni, with her sights set on taking part in the Paralympic Games, was to continue with her racing she needed her own tailor-made chair.

Even then, racing chairs were very expensive and it was the Cardiff Branch of the Rotary Club which raised the funds for Tanni to buy a state-of-the-art Bromakin racing wheelchair. In January 1987, this was handed over by John Lister and Michael Hall at a short ceremony at the YMCA in Cardiff. It was an opportunity for Tanni's current achievements to be listed, and reference was made to her British record in the wheelchair slalom achieved in 1981, to her 100 metres record at Stoke Mandeville in 1984, to her award as Junior Personality of the Year in 1985. And, to bring the list of achievements up to date, the official Rotary citation continued:

'In her first year as a senior in 1986 at the British Paraplegic Games she was first in the wheelchair slalom and received the award for the best effort by any competitor.' In those games Tanni had also taken part in events in the swimming pool.

'Rotary is delighted to assist a young lady of Tanni's ability and has confidence that she will earn further honours in the field of disabled games in the future.'

That summer Tanni was not to disappoint and success came quickly. In her new chair at the 1987 National British Paraplegic Games she won three Gold and two Silver medals and broke the British record in the 200 metres. The racing chair given to Tanni is still in use. Although it has been superseded technically by later models and designs, it is still retained by Rotary and loaned out to anyone in the area wanting to try out a racing chair and learn the basic skills.

At school, Tanni was now a well-known personality and collegues were proud to share in her achievements on the track. Jo Dutch recalls the teachers following her progress and encouraging her.

'It is not often that a school has a pupil who excels,' Jo adds, 'and many of the teachers, knowing that it would be good for the school, were keen that it should be known that Tanni was from St Cyres. As far as I remember, there was never any trouble about Tanni taking time off school to compete. What she was doing was seen by the school to be enhancing its good reputation.'

In Tanni's final year at the school her headmaster, Mr Brian Rowlands, was quoted in a local paper profile on Tanni as saying: 'It might sound a little bit over the top but I have to say that I considered it a privilege that Tanni was a pupil at my school.'

His star pupil was not only well on her way to four 'A' levels which would secure her a university place, but she had also been selected to compete in the World Games at Stoke Mandeville and then to travel on to the International Games in Vienna.

It was at Stoke Mandeville, during the Games, that Tanni celebrated her eighteenth birthday. Her parents set up a party in a field, friends were invited, a cake was produced and a bottle of Champagne was opened.

Going to Austria was Tanni's first trip abroad as an athlete and she flew from Heathrow with other members of the British Squad.

As it was the first time she had flown, Tanni was as excited about the flying as she was about competing. She raced in the 100 metres, 200 metres and 400 metres in her category, recording a

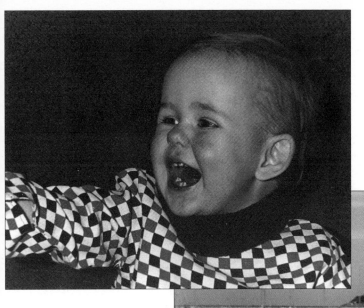

A handful from the very first moment! Tanni, pictured in her first year, bursts onto the scene.

Making the most of the good weather, on holiday in Brixham with sister Sian in 1974.

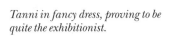

Tanni in fancy dress, proving to be quite the exhibitionist.

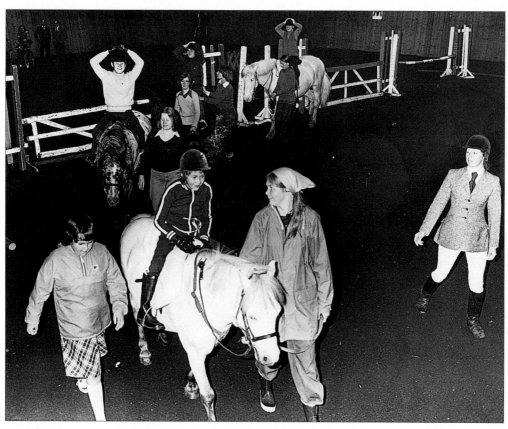

Above: Eager to try everything, Tanni on a pony at a local riding school with Sian walking alongside.

Below: Tanni was to become a sixer in Dinah Cadogan's brownie pack.

Left: Winner of the student category of The Times Sportswoman of the Year in 1988. Tanni is pictured with Olympic gold medallist Mary Peters (right).

Right: The Training and Enterprise Council used her image to inspire others through its poster campaign.

Below: Leading round a bend in the course of the Portsmouth half-marathon in 1992.

Above: A victorious Tanni salutes the crowds after her triumphant 400m semi-final at the Barcelona Paralympics in 1992.

Below: Four times at Barcelona, Tanni collects a Gold medal for Great Britain. Here she receives one for the 200m with Ingrid Lauridson of Denmark (right) in silver position and Patty Durkin of the USA (left) collecting bronze.

In 1992, Tanni becomes the first wheelchair athlete to be awarded the trophy for Welsh Sports Personality of the Year. The award is presented by Sir Anthony Hopkins.

The honours come rolling in. Here Tanni is seen with other winners of the RADAR 'People of the Year'.

Throughout the hectic year, Tanni remains involved with fundraising for disability sports. She is pictured here as one of the athletes benefitting from funds raised by the Royal Welsh Fusiliers.

THIS CENTRE WAS OPENED BY
MISS TANNI GREY, MBE
PARALYMPIC GOLD MEDALIST
ON 26TH MAY 1993.

Above: In 1993 Tanni was awarded an honorary Master of Arts degree by her old university at Loughborough.

Left: Seen holding one of its patients, Tanni opens a new PDSA clinic.

Right: Seated at an exhibition beneath her portrait by John Kent.

Below: Tanni receiving a Variety Club award in 1993 from the Duke of Edinburgh.

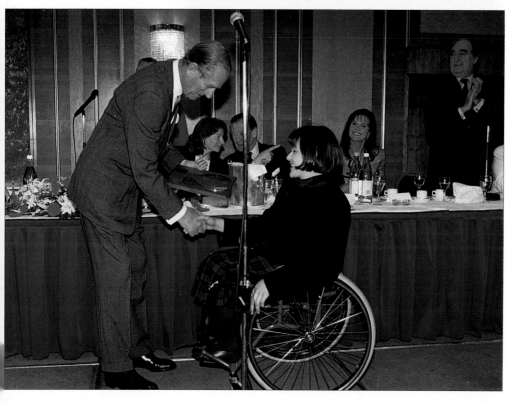

'It was a very emotional moment for us.' Tanni receives her MBE.

personal best and a new British record time of 45.37 seconds in the 200 metres.

Now, with the prospect of becoming a student at a university famed throughout the world for its sporting achievements, Tanni could look ahead to even greater success. By the summer of 1987 she had begun, with discipline and determination, to train as an athlete. In February of that year she had joined the Bridgend Athletics Club and come under the influence of the senior coach, Roy Anthony. Roy, a former policeman and middle-distance specialist, had heard about Tanni when working for the Welsh Sports Council.

He still remembers the first time Tanni was mentioned to him by his immediate boss, Marilyn Godfrey, who at the time was responsible for developing disability sport. They were at a committee meeting and she asked Roy, 'How would you like a potential Paralympic athlete to coach?'.

'You've got a handicapped kiddy, have you? A good one?' he replied.

'Yes, there's a lot of potential in this lass. She's very willing and she'll work hard.'

And so it was arranged that Tanni would come with her parents to the Bridgend club on the 18th February. Roy was impressed by Tanni's lively attitude and talked to her straight about his philosophy. He said he was a hard taskmaster and would not treat her any differently from anybody else. He would push her to her limits. Tanni agreed and Roy took her through a variety of physical routines to find out what she could do.

Visits to Bridgend then became a regular part of her life. She trained fully with the able-bodied athletes at the club.

'I have been involved with a few disabled people, but I have never pushed anybody like I pushed Tanni because they wouldn't go that far themselves,' Roy recalls. 'I would see the others put the brakes on, but Tanni appeared not to know how to do that. I might, for example, set her ten 200 metres sprints on the track with a sensible rest in between. She would get to eight and I would look at her and say "Tan, you've done enough". "No, no, no," she'd insist, "I'll do the other two." "No, Tanni, you've had enough, cool down." And I'd have to be firm with her. Being hard on an athlete involves not just pushing them to their limits, but telling them when they've gone far enough. When you know they've had enough, it is silly to push them further.'

There is however one occasion which Roy looks back on with mixed amusement and horror. Having devised some mobility exercises for Tanni, he arranged for her to come in half an hour before the main session to work on them. She was in a little room at the Bridgend Recreation Centre, out of her chair lying on her tummy on the floor, working on exercises designed to bring her shoulders back and strengthen her spine. Yet, despite Roy's encouragement, she could not move more than an inch.

Then Sulwen, who was watching, said, 'It's a bit difficult, Roy. She perhaps doesn't want to tell you, but she's got a steel rod fused into her spine.'

'Oh my God, Tanni!' Roy cried. 'Why didn't you tell me? I've been trying to turn you into a blooming 'S' hook!'

It was at Bridgend that Roy and Tanni devised the best way of taping her hands to protect them when she was training and racing at speed. At a local sports meeting they had been watching some of the more experienced athletes and took the opportunity to seek advice from them. They talked generally about training methods but it was the advice on protecting the hands that was of the greatest value to Tanni. Roy and Tanni decided that taping her thumbs was the most essential because it was her thumbs that took the brunt of the hand pressure on the moving wheels.

The great advantage to Tanni of the Bridgend regime was that it was a club which produced outstanding athletes and also retained a more relaxed and informal atmosphere. The idea of disabled and able-bodied athletes training together was still very much in its infancy.

'We did it without being conscious of it,' Roy says looking back. 'I'd say "Tanni line up there with Jo and Jack and Billy, right, on the gun, 100 metres, go." That was it. The fact that she was in a wheelchair made no difference.

'Some of the younger kids were curious and impressed at her speed, particularly when she beat them in her chair.'

Her time at Bridgend, although short, was important to her development as an athlete. It gave her her first feel for the world of top-class sport. No longer was she a schoolgirl with a particular gift. She was beginning to realize she was a young woman with an outstanding talent. Conditions at Bridgend were not ideal and Roy Anthony laments the fact that investment in facilities had not kept pace with those at some of the more glamorous sports venues in South Wales. Her weekly sessions at Bridgend involved training on grass, which was tough going.

'When the weather was bad we used to train in the car park,' Tanni remembers. 'The facilities were not great, but Bridgend had a good atmosphere and was such a fun club to be with. I loved it and was a member until I went to university. At Bridgend they didn't treated me any differently and I didn't get any weird looks.'

This experience however meant that it came as something of a shock to Tanni when she arrived at Loughborough and found a very different attitude towards her when she sought to use the top-grade facilities. It was not just Tanni who was shocked. The Loughborough athletes had never seen anyone in a wheelchair in an athletics club before, and it was beyond their comprehension that a young politics student with spina bifida, who used a wheelchair, could be a high-flying sportswoman.

CHAPTER THREE

Training with the elite

'I haven't got a problem, have you?'

A GRADUATION AT ANY university, even a twentieth-century one designated a University of Technology, is a colourful event. Traditions are carried from the historic places of learning and the principal university figures parade in their distinctive robes of office.

Loughborough's graduates are presented in conventional gown, hood and mortar board with the recipients of higher degrees wearing scarlet, gold and purple. The degree-awarding ceremony starts with the arrival of the academic procession led by the two university marshals. To the fore are the honourary graduates of the day.

It is very unusual for a university to invite one of its recent graduates back to receive an honourary degree within just a couple of years of first graduating. Yet, following Tanni's outstanding achievements at the Barcelona Paralympics, the University of Loughborough took that rare step and invited her to receive the honourary degree of Master of Arts 'for sporting excellence and services to national and international sport'.

She arrived on the familiar campus on the morning of Friday, 9 July 1993 with her parents and sister and, unlike the first occasion she graduated, she did not robe with the milling crowds of graduating students, but was taken to the special robing room reserved for the academics and honourary graduates.

That morning the University's chancellor, Sir Denis Rooke, the former chairman of British Gas, and himself the past recipient of at least four honourary degrees, was to confer two honourary marks of academic distinction. Ahead of Tanni was Professor Brian Shackel, selected to receive the degree of Doctor of Technology for his services to the University and his contribution to the establishment of ergonomics. Professor Shackel had been director of Loughborough's own Human Sciences and Advanced Technology Research Institute.

The ceremony was held in the physical education centre, the largest hall available, and the academics and robed party sat on a raised dias fronted by flowers for the ceremony. The graduands sat in the main body of the hall, rows of proud friends and family on either side. The graduands had exchanged their african violet coloured tracksuits, so prized by them as Loughborough students, for the black gowns and purple and white hoods of academic achievement.

The Chancellor's procession arrived to the accompaniment of Purcell's trumpet tune. The assembled congregation rose as the marshals led the members of the General Assembly, Senate and Council, and then the honorary graduands followed by the great and the good of the University establishment, to their seats.

The Public Orator, Dr Andrew Wilson, began his citation in honour of Tanni with the words 'One of the great advantages of working at Loughborough is that the less sporty of us are able to bask in the reflected glory of the international sportswomen and sportsmen who abound here'.

Dr Wilson then continued with a summary of Tanni's sporting achievements, taking the listening audience through her first interest in a wide variety of sports to her Barcelona Paralympic triumph, spicing the information with wry humour.

'Nobody should foster any illusions about the intensity of competition at this level. These are world-class athletes training hard and competing hard for something that they value highly. Unsporting behaviour is resented as bitterly in her sport as in any other. One competitor who manipulated a race recently, and exploited his fellow competitors, found himself dumped out of his chair on his next race. Spanners in wheels are not unknown.

'To be the holder of four world records, to have four gold medals, to be the first woman under one minute for the 400 metres – these all mark her out as a sportswoman of great distinction. Throughout all of this she has been strongly supported by her family. Her parents have always believed that there is nothing that she can't do, and she has proved them right.'

Then, turning to Tanni's parents seated in the hall, Dr Wilson added, 'She has inherited her mother's bloody-mindedness!'.

He then rounded off his address in these terms.

'Tanni is very down to earth about her achievements. When people tell her that she is very brave, she responds by saying that she is very stupid. How else do you explain the demanding training schedule and the sheer lunacy of marathons.

'Tanni is very down to earth about being a wheelchair-user. She is irritated by people who see the chair rather than the person, but views it as their problem, not hers. Tanni is not a woman to be pushed around.

'Tanni says that this honorary degree is about the only way she would get an MA. I doubt that. I think that if she wanted one through academic study, she'd get it. But now she is a full-time athlete – it beats working.'

Then Tanni came forward up the ramp, constructed for the occasion, on to the platform, and the towering figure of Sir Denis Rooke came forward to shake her hand.

On her visit to the campus that day Tanni took the opportunity to update herself on some of the university's work studying the science of Paralympic sports. Loughborough has a sport and disability research group made up of a sociologist, sports nutritionist, physiotherapist and a sports physiologist. Its objectives are to generate, collect, store and disseminate knowledge on sport and disability. The university has collaborated with a range of British and European disability sports organizations and its work to date has included a number of multi-disciplinary studies on subjects ranging from nutrition to sports injuries, even to the 'sub culture' of wheelchair racing.

The television company, Pilgrim Productions Canterbury, was

making a documentary for BBC 2 and filmed Tanni using some of the equipment. Sessions of her racing on static rollers and having her intake of air monitored made good footage. It was a session similar to Tanni's own more serious testing undertaken at Crewe and Manchester Metropolitan University.

On the day of her graduation as an honorary Master of Arts, Loughborough felt a very different place to Tanni from what she had encountered as a first year student in 1987. Little could she have realized then that her own sporting achievements would have such an impact on the institution that it would encourage a serious interest in the study of disability sport.

Certainly there is no doubt that it has been largely Tanni's achievements and her close associations with the university, and the pride the university has taken in her achievements, which have spurred Loughborough into taking a serious look at this growing field of sporting activity.

Yet when Tanni first sought to take part as an athlete in the full training sessions at Loughborough, not only were the other athletes surprised and amazed, but the facilities were ill-prepared for such a request.

When it was suggested, early on, that it might be better if Tanni trained on the track at a different time, away from the able-bodied athletes, Tanni's reaction was: 'I haven't got a problem, have you?'.

Tanni also found that her requirements conflicted with those of the main group in the gymnasium. It was difficult for her to join in with 150 specimens of able-bodied perfection, a high proportion of them in their international kit, their GB tops, all doing leg exercises when she wanted to exercise her arms. Common procedures, such as sit-ups, were not possible for Tanni, so indoor-circuit training also proved a problem. On the track the runners were unused to having a wheelchair around.

Today, at her Cardiff club, Tanni is a familiar sight on the track. Other athletes are happy to train with her and some no doubt are a little in awe of her achievements and reputation as an international sportswoman.

There was a further difficulty at Loughborough in that the track was not easily accessible and Tanni often found it difficult to get a key. As none of Tanni's immediate friends at Loughborough was a runner she would often have to wait for a stranger or security officer to let her on and off the track. Tanni did not meet the other athletes in the normal course of her daily studies and for a long while she had no social contact with them.

The solution in the end was relatively simple. Two of Tanni's friends, who were studying civil engineering, were keen mountaineers and Tanni decided to join the Loughborough mountaineers on their circuit-training sessions. The group of fifteen was small and manageable and had access to the same large gymnasium. Tanni now had room to try out a range of equipment and because the mountaineers were keen to develop their arms as much as their legs, she was able to fit in with their training routines far more easily. She also felt that their attitude to her was much better and began to train comfortably alongside them.

She was very glad to have found a way of keeping up her training without the strains of feeling that she was the odd one out in a rather unwelcoming group.

'To be honest, I think any university that I'd gone to at that time would have been the same. The attitudes I came up against made me realize, time and again, that in some way I was different.'

Of course it is always the case that anyone with a disability is conspicuous and any mishap that befalls a wheelchair-user can be especially embarrassing if it happens in public. Tanni still blushes at the memory of the day she fell headlong from her chair on the campus.

'I was training one Wednesday afternoon when I had my first three-wheel chair and I hit a tiny little bump or hole in the road. My chair went one way and I went the other, smacking my head on the ground. I remember looking at my arm and there was blood all down my right shoulder. I just lay on the floor thinking, "Oh, my god, who's seen me?". People charged over and were really worried. I had also hit my face, so there was blood there too. I remember lying there, embarrassed because I'd crashed.'

When Tanni went back to her room and looked in the mirror, her face was bruised and swollen. Her parents were due to visit the next day so Tanni rang to warn them that she had had a 'bit of a crash, but it's okay, just a small scratch'.

The next morning, however, Tanni could not see out of her left eye which was black and closed. When her mother saw her she was taken back, but then started laughing. Tanni was not going to get much sympathy from the family, especially when she had to admit how the accident had happened. No, she said, she wasn't with anyone and she wasn't in a pack racing.

'I hit this lump of grass on the road,' she admitted. Hardly a glamorous way to sustain such a conspicuous injury!

Aside from the initial attitude of some of the Loughborough athletes, Tanni found the university welcoming and accommodating. It made sure, for instance, that she could live on campus, appreciating that finding lodgings or a flat in the area with suitable access might have been difficult. One of the bungalows at the base of a twenty-one storey tower block was converted for her use. Tanni does not normally need a specially adapted bathroom, but the conversion work meant that there would be a place on campus for future disabled students.

There was one problem, however, in that the bungalow was not part of the main 'Towers' hall and Tanni sometimes felt a little isolated. To get in to Towers, where friends and other student facilities were to be found, Tanni had to negotiate steps. And to gain access to a higher floor she had to use one of two lifts, each of which only stopped at every other floor. This meant that if she wanted to go to see someone in a room on one of the even-numbered floors she had to take the lift on the east side. Similarly, to visit an odd-numbered floor, she had to take a lift on the west side. Even then she sometimes had internal steps to negotiate.

'If, for example, I wanted to get to West 7 to visit a friend I could either go up ten steps on the west side and then up in the lift or choose to go up the east side lift to floor 8 and down a flight. It was complicated!'

Thus it was, to counteract these problems, that within a couple of weeks of arriving at Loughborough Tanni had devised a new system for getting up and down steps with her chair. One day she wanted to see a friend on the seventh floor and there was no one around to help.

'So,' she said, 'I found a way of getting up the steps on my bum and dragging my chair as I did so. Once I'd done this a few times it got relatively easy.

'Also, because there were over 300 people in the Hall, there was usually someone about to pick up the chair and throw it up the steps. There were also a couple of strong guys in my first year who would carry me around. Going up to the bar of the refectory with a group of friends was certainly not a problem – they would carry me. Of course, there were a few people who were a bit stand-offish, probably because they had never seen a wheelchair before.'

Tanni made a wide range of friends at Loughborough, but one friendship in particular evolved into something deeper and more intimate. Andy was a fellow student who became especially fond of Tanni and she of him. He was more than willing to offer an extra hand and, as time went by, was increasingly seen by her side. He also came to know Sulwen and Peter and they liked him very much. He was not Tanni's first boyfriend – she had been very popular at school – but, for a while, he was especially close to her.

During her first year at Loughborough Tanni accepted almost every challenge she was offered. Thus it was that, one freezing cold April day, she found herself plunged in a pool in full scuba diving kit.

'I was going across the campus one day and a bloke came up to me and said "Do you fancy taking up scuba diving?" "Yeah,' I said, "all right. I'll give it a go". I tried it out in the pool, we had to be tied together because when they planned to go they wouldn't be able to see more than three feet in front under water. It certainly wasn't my idea of what scuba diving was. I'd have much preferred the Mediterranean or the Great Barrier Reef, not somewhere, as planned, off the east coast of Scotland.

'I quickly found that I hated it. I was terrified of being under water, and the tank on my back caused me problems. Also because I had no weight in my legs or control over them, I had to have added weights on my hips and ankles. I had so much stuff, it used to take me an hour to get ready, and afterwards the bottom of my spine would hurt.'

Tanni and scuba diving parted company.

Going to university always involves getting used to a new way of life and a self-disciplined regime of study, lectures, seminars and essay-writing. Tanni also needed to adapt to a subject she had not studied at school – her degree in politics was not her first choice.

Introductions to sociology, psychology and economics were included in the first year and, in particular, Tanni found economics a difficult topic to grasp. As no one in her group had studied economics before she recalls very few of them having any idea as to what the subject was about. She turned up to every lecture, but hated the subject.

Opting for politics had not been prompted by Tanni holding any strong political views. She was interested in the mechanisms of politics and the systems of government, but did not consider herself a political animal. She found, by contrast however, that the majority of people on her course were very politically aware. Today her interests are very much in the internal politics of the Paralympic movement, but as far as wider political events are concerned Tanni has not nailed her colours firmly to any mast. She is not interested in or impressed by British party politics and sees herself as a Green with a keen awareness of environmental issues.

Academically, Tanni enjoyed her first year at Loughborough, even though she admits that she did not do brilliantly well and that her knowledge, or rather her lack of knowledge of economics let her down.

For undergraduates the social life on and off the campus is, of course, just as important as the degree course. Tanni took full advantage of the opportunities to enjoy herself. She had a car – a specially adapted Vauxhall Astra – and was in many ways more mobile than some of her friends.

One of the difficulties drivers with disabilities face is filling up with petrol. Self-service pumps are now so common that finding an attendant to fill the tank is difficult. Whenever she can, Tanni fills up at a local petrol station which still provides its customers with a refuelling service. If, however, she is away from base she has to get out of the car into her day chair and serve herself. Her chair travels everywhere with. Its wheels detach and it can be easily stored away in the car so that Tanni can lift it out and reassemble it before lifting herself into it from the driver's seat.

In addition to the study and social side of university, Tanni also had to fit in her sports training. Fortunately, by the second year, when she not only became an international competitor but was also selected to fill a coveted place at the Seoul Paralympics in 1988, there was a sea-change in the other Loughborough athletes' attitudes towards Tanni.

Also important in raising the profile of disability sport at the university was the fact that the campus hosted the National Disabled Student Games. Sponsored by the Midland Bank over the weekend of 15-17 April 1988, nearly 260 competitors took part in the games of that year together with 75 officials and 120 student volunteers. In addition with many friends, relations and other spectators present, the competition was a major event.

The Games saw the breaking of 47 women's and 36 men's games records. Tanni herself caught the attention of competitors and spectators with her victories in the 60 metres and 100 metres in new Games' record times. She broke the similar record in the wheelchair slalom. Her winning times were 14 seconds for the 60 metres and 22 seconds in the 100 metres and 1 minute 43.7 seconds in the slalom. Tanni received her winners' medals from the television sports presenter Harry Carpenter.

Reviewing the event, the Loughborough Students' Community Action Group noted how, despite the wet weather, the feedback from everyone involved had been very positive.

Tanni herself remembers that 'it all happened during the vacation and was like a reunion with many friends coming back to help. It was all good fun with serious sport alongside those of other standards.

'The hosting of the National Disabled Student Games,' Tanni believes, 'helped change a few people's opinions of disability sport and certainly Loughborough is now very interested. Attitudes everywhere seem to have evolved over the last ten years. If I was being cynical I would suggest that this is because there are papers to be written, conferences to attend, and a lot of money in disabled sport at an academic level. There is also a lot of kudos to be had from being a college specializing in this field.'

Six weeks after the Games, the letter which Tanni had been hoping for and working towards throughout all her hours of training, arrived at her home address in Wales. With the logo of the 1988 Seoul Paralympics at the top left-hand corner and the address of the British Paralympic Committee on the right, it brought the long-awaited news that she had been selected as a competitor at the very highest level. Above the signatures of Bob Price, Head of Delegation and Tony Sainsbury, Team Manager, the letter began:

> *Dear Tanni, We offer you our warmest congratulations on being selected for the Great Britain Paralympic team competing in Seoul, South Korea, in October 1988. You will be competing in Athletics.*

And, after giving details about acceptance of the invitation and the relevant documents, the letter finished:

> *Best wishes with your training programme and in your quest for Gold.*

Tanni's reaction on opening the letter was 'Wow!' She had taken part in training and trials and knew that she had reached the required standard in her events and class, but she knew that her selection was not a foregone conclusion. There was only one place for a British woman in her events and she had a rival. Behind the scenes, as she now knows from her own experience of the administration of sport, officials would have been fighting for places. Britain had only been allocated a certain number of places and these had to be ruthlessly divided between the various disability groups and events, with the single goal of maximizing Britain's medal potential. This naturally resulted in tension between the different disciplines. Some people were bound to be disappointed and before Tanni read the letter confirming her selection she was only too aware of this.

As it was, the news was good. Tanni's career was taking off. That summer she was also chosen to go to Arlington, Texas, to compete in the Nautilus International Wheelchair Classic, a top American wheelchair challenge in the three sprint events at which she was now specializing, the 100, 200 and 400 metres. Her results showed her international class, but were not the best indicator as to her form for Seoul. She won Bronze medals in the two shorter distances and came fifth in the 400 metres. She also became established as a member of the British Squad having been chosen to take part in its special training schedule in the more reliable weather of Portugal. Her jet-setting years had begun.

'Going to America on my first long-haul flight was tremendously exciting. As well as competing we saw the sites. I went to Southfork, the ranch from the soap opera *Dallas*. It was very disappointing, nothing like what I had expected from seeing it on television.'

Within a couple of days of her selection for the Seoul Squad Tanni found that there is more involved in being a Paralympian than merely training for and competing in her chosen events. She had become a personality in the sport and a representative of it. On 27 May the British Paralympic Sports Society asked her to be one of the ten representatives of the Seoul team to travel to the Cirencester Park Polo Club in aid of the BPSS appeal fund for the Paralympic Games. She was to be at the club on 4 June at 12 noon, wearing her GB tracksuit, to meet those present – among them would be the Prince of Wales who was also one of the polo players competing for the Dorchester trophy.

Other letters arrived at her home, one from Richard Jones, headmaster of Erw'r Delyn school in Penarth.

> *Dear Tanni,*
>
> *All too often in my professional life a telephone call from a parent means a problem or some trouble to be smoothed over. Not last Friday when your Mum called in a state of some excitement! Your selection for the Olympic team is great news, many many congratulations. The right combination of talent, physical prowess and determination along with tremendous back-up from coaches and Mum and Dad has all gone to achieve a just reward.*
>
> *Of course, now that the Champagne bubbles have settled, you will be aware that being chosen is one thing, winning comes next!*

And an all important note arrived in June from Loughborough University not only offering the University's congratulations on her selection but approving Tanni's request for leave of absence during the first three weeks of the term so that she could participate.

A key factor in her competing at Seoul would be, of course, the availability of a top-class chair. The one she used for racing was her Bromakin, but for the slalom she would need a new chair suitable for the Paralympics.

By July an order was placed with the Greenbank project, a co-operative in Liverpool which specialized in the production of the type of chair that Tanni would need. It was an expensive item, the total coming to £972, but the money was raised from sponsors and donations: £100 came from the South Wales Association for Spina Bifida and Hydrocephalus; £25 arrived from Lloyds Bank; £250 was given by South Wales Electricity (after Sulwen had had a particularly persuasive conversation with the company's public relations manager); Welsh Water chipped in with £25; and St Cyres Sixth Form sent a cheque for a similar amount.

South Glamorgan County Council also came up trumps with a grant for £400 towards her participation in the October Games, even though the date of the letter on behalf of the Chief Executive offering the sum was not sent until November.

The chair, when it arrived was the most modern available but today, only seven years on, the racing chair Tanni used at Seoul look as outdated as an Austin Seven sitting next to the latest Vauxhall Astra. None of the steering devices projecting forward were included in the design and the sports chair, even though of a souped-up variety, still looks like a day chair.

It might be supposed that getting ready to compete in the Paralympic Games is solely a matter of being well trained, talented and having the right equipment, but the organizational complications, are further hurdles to overcome.

First of all, there are health matters to bear in mind, with the team doctor advising on strongly recommended inoculations. Then the uniform has to be ordered and fitted. For 'walking out' at the Paralympic Games this consisted of a blazer with a Union Jack badge, a skirt, two blouses, a cravat, a pair of shoes and two pairs of socks. Added to this was the tracksuit, leisure suit, rain suit and such miscellaneous items as a sweater, two T-shirts and a bag to carry everything in. Tanni also had to take care of details such as her passport and how to get a supply of pocket money, in Korean Won, of which there were then around 1500 to the £1.

The team was given a high-profile sendoff with the Princess of Wales present in her capacity as Patron of the British Sports Association for the Disabled. Boxer Frank Bruno and swimmer Duncan Goodhew were also there to wish the competitors well.

To prepare the team for Seoul and to send it on its way had cost £250,000, raised jointly by five disability organizations. The then Minister of Sport, Colin Moynihan, had raised £10,000 of that sum personally by means of a sponsored cycle ride.

The Paralympics, which had evolved into the major event in Seoul 1988, had started from modest beginnings. They were the brain-child of Sir Ludwig Guttmann who, in 1948, was the director of the National Spinal Injuries Centre at Stoke

Mandeville Hospital, Aylesbury. The idea at the start was that through competitive sport young men and women who had sustained spinal injuries and lost the use of the lower parts of their body, could develop renewed self-esteem and derive considerable therapeutic value. Initially the majority of participants were British servicemen disabled during the Second World War, but in due course disabled sport expanded to include other disabilities and other nations.

Since 1960 the Olympics of disabled athletes had taken place, whenever possible, at or close to the venue of the Olympic Games. The planning for the Seoul Games had started in 1982 just as Tanni herself was trying wheelchair sport for the first time. The procedure was that the Stoke Mandeville Games Federation approached the organizers of disabled sport in Korea asking them to set up a committee to investigate the possibilities of staging the Paralympic Games in conjunction with the Olympics. The organizers were only too aware of the problems involved as, in 1980, the Games had to be switched to the Netherlands amidst the political problems of staging the Olympics in the Soviet Union; and, in 1984, the World Wheelchair Games were switched at the last minute to Stoke Mandeville and hosted by the British when arrangements in America broke down.

The Seoul Games attracted 4000 competitors from 65 countries, including 240 from Britain, in a wide range of athletics events and classes. In total, 16 sports were represented. For those present it was all absorbing but for the outside world the Games, happening in a far-off place, were of only marginal significance. Some of the British newspapers carried short reports amounting to a dozen or so column inches a day, but compared with the saturation coverage of the Olympic Games on radio, television and in the press, the Paralympics received scant attention.

It was perhaps indicative that the Games were slowly emerging from being merely therapeutic Games for handicapped people to being sporting events in their own right, that it was made clear from the start that the Paralympians would be subjected to the same tests for illegal drugs as their able-bodied colleagues. Thus, for the first time in the twenty-eight year history of the Paralympic Games, officials were safeguarding themselves against a potential Ben Johnson style scandal. It was acknowledged, however, that disabled athletes, found to test positive, could provide an adequate defence by showing a valid medical certificate indicating that the drugs taken were prescribed for their condition.

The Paralympic village, set up in a southern suburb of the Korean capital, included over 1300 apartments, nearly 500 of which were designed for wheelchair-users. Security was strict and police were often seen accompanying wheelchair athletes out training. The atmosphere in the village was festive with buildings festooned with flags and balloons.

Tanni's immediate impressions of Seoul were penned in a card posted to her parents and grandmother. Having reported a successful but tiring flight and the fact that she had had her passport stamped in Alaska, she then went on to describe her reception at the airport:

Brilliant. I was given a huge bunch of roses. Trip to village – good. We had a police escort and we didn't need to stop at any red lights. Very well organised. Accommodation excellent. All designed for chairs. I don't think it's the same village as the ABs [able bodied] but its design is similar, I'll check on that. I'm on the eleventh floor at the moment and sharing with Alison Bennie, swimming and Moira, they're getting moved tomorrow. Weather is beautiful although it does get a bit cold at night. The people are amazingly friendly. They stop you all the time to speak to you and want to know where you come from. The security is quite tight. Today I went for a walk around the perimeter and all of a sudden all these whistles blew and about three guards rushed after me. They wanted to know what I was doing. After I told them, there was no hassle – all they wanted to do was practise their English on me.

Tomorrow I'm going to sort out my wheelchair. At the moment the box is in the basement. I'll have to find some people to bring it up. At the moment I'm in my room. It's about 7 pm but it's lovely. Getting over the jet lag wasn't too bad, it may be worse the other way. Loads of people brought Union Jacks. They hung them over the balcony. I didn't think of that. It looks very smart from the outside. I've now been here two days, it's 11.30 pm. The Aussies, Canadians, Yanks, Brazilians, French and Italians have arrived. Korea came today. Their team is huge. I found out where to buy the cheap gear and I'm hopefully going tomorrow. They also do stitched jackets. I'm going to try and get one with the five Paralympic symbols on the back and 'Tanni Grey British Paralympic Track Team '88' written on (if I can find a shop). It's so noisy here, I doubt I'll sleep. It's too hot to shut the window but that lets the noise in. I found out how to phone home and I think they've got a fax here. If I can I'll send you one to give you an idea of when I can ring. Went to the track today. Not the stadium but fairly near. Apparently this is not the Olympic village, that's about ten minutes away. It's huge this. Isn't too bad. I'm sure we can survive. Anyway no more paper – I'll write again. Miss you all, lots of love Tanni.

After Tanni's first two room-mates had left she found herself sharing accommodation with two of the basketball team, one of whom was Tracey Lewis, later to become one of her main opponents on the track.

At that time Tracey did not have a race chair of her own, but was thinking very seriously of saving up for one and becoming a track athlete. She spent as much spare time as she could watching the track events at the stadium and deciding in her own mind that she had the chance of becoming one of the leading woman athletes, certainly in the T3 classification. She talked to Tanni about this when they met from time to time in the room and over meals. She found Tanni helpful, but not close. She recognized the competitive side of Tanni's nature and put the slight distance in their relationship down to a feeling that Tanni might not want a rival.

'I thought she would have welcomed me on the basis that the more competitors there are, the better the competition and the more satisfying victory when it comes,' Tracey now says.

Life in the village was serious and disciplined. Everybody had made such an effort to get selected, no one was going to misbehave.

Even the athletes who had finished their events, either knocked out at an early stage or triumphant, and wanting to drown their sorrows or shout from the roof-tops, realized it would be unfair to disturb the concentration of others by letting off steam.

The opening ceremony took place in the main Olympic stadium, built at a cost of £57 million and set in a 270-acre park. As with the Olympic Games, the ceremony centred around a parade of athletes and the lighting of a Paralympic torch.

'It was amazing to be part of it,' Tanni said, 'even though we had to wait up to five hours in a field outside to get in. Yes, by then, we were hot and tired and yet as soon as we went up and over the little ramp into the stadium the atmosphere was incredible. There were 60,000 people cheering.'

The atmosphere changed somewhat, however, after the euphoria of the opening event. When Tanni came to take part in her first heat, the stadium seemed virtually empty. There were indeed many spectators – far more than Tanni had ever competed in front of before – but because the stadium was so huge it swallowed them up.

Tanni succeeded in getting through to the finals in all her events, and came third in the 400 metres. She went to the podium to receive her medal with its Paralympic logo and picture of the stadium imprinted on one side and red, yellow, blue and white ribbon attached.

To win a Bronze was not a disappointment and to underline the achievement she recorded a new British record of 81 seconds in the 400 metres. In the final medals table her Bronze, one of fifty-one collected by Britain, helped put her country in third place, behind the United States and West Germany.

Back home in Wales, Sulwen and Peter had heard little news through the media. They knew that Tanni had arrived safely and they had had a long telephone conversation with her on the

Saturday when a number of things were bothering her about her timetable of events. 'She was in a right strop,' Sulwen recalls. She ended the call, however, saying she would phone again if she won anything.

It was 4 am in the morning when the telephone rang. Sulwen took the call in the bedroom and Sian quickly came in, guessing it was Tanni calling from Korea. A chirpy familiar voice was on the line.

'Hi Mum, it's Tan. I've won a Bronze.'

Early next morning the news spread like wildfire through South Wales, with Sulwen calling the local radio station to give them the news about Tanni and Chris Hallam who had also won a Bronze for Wales.

Tanni's achievement, a British record broken, could have been seen as small beer in the context of 603 world records being established. But Tanni's success did not go unnoticed – as she was to discover on her return home.

More than half of the Gold medals won by Great Britain were away from the stadium. Twenty-three Gold, thirty-eight Silver and twenty-two Bronze medals, a total of eighty-three were won by the swimmers. There was a table-tennis Gold, one for snooker, one for shooting, one for judo, one for fencing, two for archery and three for lawn bowling. Paul Noble won three Gold and three Silver medals as a swimmer. Mike Kenny did even better with five Gold medals and a Silver. Bob Matthews won three Gold medals as did Beverley Gull, to name just a few of the outstanding achievers.

The British Paralympic Association celebratory handbook of the Seoul Paralympics listed all the medal winners and Bob Price, the Head of Delegation, declared himself 'genuinely delighted with the performance of the team and truly proud to have been able to play a small part in their success'.

At the end of the event, amidst fireworks and fanfare, the flame of the VIIIth and largest Paralympic Games to date was extinguished in a ceremony every bit as lavish as that held for the Olympic Games.

'The Koreans have established the fact that the Paralympics are on a par with the Olympics,' Colin Moynihan, the British Minister for Sport declared on a visit to Seoul. 'It's long overdue, and this means that future Paralympics will have to match the new expectations. It will be tough for those who follow.'

It is difficult to assess what the long-term influence of hosting the Games had on Korea. In common with a number of far eastern countries a positive image of disability fits uneasily into the Korean culture. When asked for his impression of the Paralympic Games, one Korean taxi driver drew a finger down his cheek, tracing the tracks of imaginary tears. To him, a typical Korean, the idea of disabled people competing in athletics was a sad one.

One syndicated correspondent, based in Seoul at the time, said: 'Korea has traditionally treated its maimed and crippled, its deaf and blind, with shame. Parents of disabled children cannot arrange profitable marriages for them or hope to enjoy a comfortable old age on their offspring's salaries. To many Koreans the best place for the handicapped is out of sight and out of mind.'

At that time, it was estimated that South Korea had almost a million blind and disabled people living in the country, and the lack of services for them had drawn increasing criticism. Indeed, in June 1988, several hundred disabled people had organized a protest claiming that the staging of the Paralympics in Seoul was the rulers' way of assuaging guilt without doing anything to assist the country's disabled people themselves.

As a student of politics it was Tanni's first opportunity to witness at first hand a country emerging from developing to industrial status. During her time in Seoul, she therefore took the opportunity to see more of the country.

Along with three friends, she hired a bus for a couple of days and toured Seoul and the surrounding area. They visited the sites of the royal palaces and went up to the de-militarized zone, seeing a culture so different for their own that it was an eye-opener for all of them. Away from the tourist traps Tanni and her friends witnessed a great deal of poverty with people begging on the streets and large numbers of young girls plying their trade as prostitutes in the red-light district. She learned that the attitude of many ordinary Koreans towards Americans was far from friendly and that, for this reason, British Paralympians were advised to wear their British tracksuits when travelling around. She noticed that the Canadians, easily mistaken for Americans in every other way, never went outside the Paralympic villages without a conspicuous red maple-leaf tracksuit on view.

Up until that time Tanni, then aged eighteen, had grown up in a culture where American influence was common. She had watched American films on television, had visited the country, and was very surprised to find such strong anti-American feelings in Korea.

If Tanni and her friends had not made a special effort to see the Korea, which was not on official view, their image of the host country would have been very limited. Up until that time, whenever they travelled from the village to the stadium not only were they taken in buses but all the traffic on the streets was stopped and a police escort raced them through all the red lights.

Their unofficial tour also brought them into contact with the life many disabled people were destined to lead in Korea.

'We saw disabled people begging on the streets – and that was very distressing.

'When we went to the main shopping areas we were treated well because the Koreans knew that we had money to spend and that there were substantial profits to be made from the Paralympic Games. Leather jackets and many clothes were very cheap compared to the prices they demand in Britain.'

Tanni found bartering at market stalls exciting, but felt rather squeamish at some of the more colourful sights, including a street-corner traditional pharmacist boiling live hedgehogs to make medicine. She also noticed that when shopkeepers and stall-holders realized that she was British, not American, prices for almost everything dropped almost immediately.

At the border between Communist North Korea and the Capitalist South Tanni was less surprised by the border guards and the barbed wire than she was by the monuments to many thousands of American soldiers who had been killed in defending the line. Having tagged on to the back of an American tour, the group heard how hundreds of thousands of American soldiers had been killed.

'How many Koreans died?' one of the group asked.

The reply shocked Tanni.

'Oh I don't know a couple of million I think.'

The young British athletes were also struck by how militarized the country was. There were American or Korean soldiers every-where it seemed.

'It gave me a different view of the world. It made me look out from the little protected world I'd been living in – and would probably still live in. It made me realize that there are so many people out there that I know nothing about.'

Arriving back in Britain there were numerous messages and letters of congratulation for Tanni from friends, colleagues, backers and sponsors. Aquascutum, the fashion company, who had paid the travelling expenses of a number of competitors, including Tanni, sent her a bouquet of flowers. The media however was somewhat muted. The return of the Paralympians, Sian remembers, was rather overshadowed by a running news story about a stranded whale.

As well as sending congratulations St Cyres, proud of its former pupil's achievements, also nominated Tanni for a *Sunday Times* Sportswomen of the Year award. The aim of this award was to honour bravery, determination, excellence and sporting spirit and to acclaim those who were making breakthroughs in increased participation of women in sport.

As the British representative in the 100, 200 and 400 metres and the slalom events at Seoul, and Bronze medal winner and British record-holder, Tanni's curriculum vitae was easy to write.

The award ceremony was sponsored by Moet and Chandon and the Central Council of Physical Recreation, and was due to be held at the Fishmonger's Hall in London on 16 November, not long after Tanni's return. Not surprisingly, given the sponsor, Tanni has kept the label of the Champagne bottle that was opened on this occasion, for there was much to celebrate. In the student category, Tanni Grey of Loughborough University was declared the winner.

Getting to London to receive the award from Olympic Gold medallist, Mary Peters, and the editor of the *Sunday Times*, Andrew Neil, required Tanni catching a train from Loughborough at 5 am, a feat of dedication which the *Sunday Times* noted with almost as much prominence as her sports achievements. Her award was a medal and a £100 voucher for sports equipment. Tanni's nomination had actually been made at the time of her selection to the Great Britain Squad, not after she came home with a Bronze. She went to the ceremony expecting to be just one of the makeweights.

'It came,' she was quoted as saying at the time, 'as a great shock to receive the award.'

The award, which could have been given to either a disabled or able-bodied athlete, was seen as special recognition for disabled sport.

'It means that disabled athletes are beginning to be recognized as sportsmen and women and not merely as disabled athletes,' Tanni said.

The honours circuit was beginning to hot up. On 19 January Tanni was invited to a reception at Lancaster House to meet the Prime Minister. On 3 February she was a key guest of the *Western Mail* at the Welsh Sports Personality of the Year awards in Cardiff, and found herself lining up with athlete, Colin Jackson, and reigning World Outdoor Bowls Singles' champion, Janet Ackland, to receive the acclaim of the audience. She received the first *Western Mail* Disabled Sports Personality of the Year award specifically for her 400 metres Bronze at Seoul.

Then, two weeks later, Tanni was one of the guests of the Lord Mayor of Cardiff at a civic dinner in honour of all the Seoul Olympic and Paralympic athletes from Wales.

One event that Tanni did not attend, however, was the dinner held by the Sports Aid Foundation with the Duchess of York present. This was to celebrate the best of British at Seoul and, it was reported that all the medal winners from the Olympic and Paralympic Games were asked. One grudging newspaper columnist then observed that no Gold medal winners had turned up to join a number of Silver and Bronze winners. The omission, it was suggested, was a display of bad politics by sport which had, that year, received £120,000 from the Foundation. As one of the medal winners from Seoul, Tanni felt she was entitled to reply and wrote a letter to the paper:

'The comments are unfair ... contrary to belief, I as an athlete do realize 'which side of my bread is buttered'. As one of the two bronze medal winners from the Paralympic team – which also won a gold – I would have gladly attended a luncheon held in our honour if only I'd received an invitation.'

The letter reflected not so much Tanni's own sense of slight, but an annoyance at an ill-informed piece of journalism.

Many sportsmen and women receive fifteen minutes of fame and these are often followed by one-off awards or dinner with the mayor. Success is always sweet and the first taste of success particularly so. Tanni, however, believed that she was only just embarking on her Paralympic career and that, with more training and further intense concentration, she could be among the Gold medal winners. She was also beginning to notice that the public perception of disability sport was changing and that a new breed of specialist elite sportsmen and women were emerging to meet this interest. She knew she had the potential to be included at the very top echelon of her sport.

At Loughborough, where many of the able-bodied elite were studying and training, Tanni returned to find an interesting change of mind and heart. Following her selection to – and success with – the Paralympic team, the top athletes at the university had started to take note of her and her reputation was now much enhanced. The fact that she had also received the prestigious *Sunday Times* award put the icing on the cake.

Perhaps with an eye to a professional future in disabled sport, Tanni, at the beginning of 1989, cut out and kept in an album the following small paragraph from a Sunday newspaper magazine:

It is nearly impossible to sum up the total earnings of athletic stars: as well as sponsorship and prize earnings, most of the stars are actually paid every time they make a track appearance. The record of their appearances outside Europe is not readily available; however, top of the British league, Steve Cram, Fatima Whitbread, and Linford Christie all have six figure earnings.

The change in tone of newspaper headlines relating to her achievements was certainly noticeable at this time. No longer was she 'plucky little student' but the 'fastest British woman on wheels' and 'Paralympic medal winner'. The potential was certainly there for Tanni to reach and get even greater success. She began planning her training schedule, looking ahead to the Barcelona Games of 1992, and had a full summer of competition arranged, including both sprints and long- distance races.

'I had my photo in the student newspaper and a huge surprise party was held for me in the Towers which was amazing. I'd come back in the middle of the week and that Friday a couple of friends said 'Let's go up to the bar'. As I was shattered I said I didn't want to go and would rather crash out in bed. They, however, told me I had to go and I walked into this huge party.'

Tanni was now widely accepted as an athlete, and a top-class one at that. She had achieved what so many of her fellow athletes at Loughborough longed to do, to represent her country at the very highest level and return with a medal.

Then, out of the blue, the unthinkable happened. For some time, Tanni had realized that things were not quite as they should be in her back where the rod had been placed at the age of thirteen. But, despite the pain, she had continued to train and compete. She knew that something would have to be done, but the decision as to when and how was taken out of her hands. In a class at university the rod in her back suddenly snapped.

CHAPTER FOUR

Disasters and doctors

*'I know as an athlete I could raise an awful lot more
money for myself if I went out and raised money as
"Tanni Grey – the poor little cripple" but I want to be
sponsored as an athlete or I'm not interested.'*

*I*T WAS NOT, to be precise, so much that the rod broke but rather
that the clip to which it was attached at the bottom end of the
spine snapped away from the bone. A bone graft, which had been
taken from Tanni's hip during the previous operation, had come
away from the spine.

Tanni was sitting in a lecture at the time and noticed a sharp
pain. When she tried to move the pain increased.

'The lecture on the European Community budget was fifteen
feet above my head and I didn't have a clue what the lecturer was
going on about, or so it seemed at the time. We had seats which
swivelled from side to side and I was playing around on mine,
basically bored, when I felt a really terrible twinge of pain. When
I got in my wheelchair at the end of the lecture, the pain got
worse and worse. I went down to tea, but the pain became
excruciating. I then went to bed, but it didn't go away.'

She had only been back at college for ten days, after a break of
six weeks, and another long period of illness and an operation
was the last thing she wanted.

Having been sick throughout the night and finding that she
could hardly move, she knew this was no minor setback and that
something was seriously wrong. In the morning she was taken to
the medical centre at Loughborough and became increasingly

ill as her spine became infected. This was potentially very dangerous, because if an infection spreads all along the spinal column it can reach the brain with dire consequences.

The Loughborough medical centre was out of its depth. The medical staff, used to treating sports injuries and conditions which strike down the able-bodied, now had a very specialist medical problem on their hands. The doctor diagnosed a chest infection – which Tanni disagreed with – and prescribed a minimum dose of antibiotics. The pain however was becoming increasingly severe.

'Even though I was paralysed and could actually feel the rod coming out at the bottom of my spine, they wouldn't transfer me to the hospital or get X-rays done. They said that there was nothing major wrong with me.'

At this stage Peter and Sulwen, who were in Cardiff, had little inkling of what was going on. And even when a friend of Tanni's telephoned and told them that Tanni was not well and had been taken to the medical centre, all they initially suspected was an attack of flu. Sulwen however, perhaps through a mother's intuition, sensed that she and Peter should go to Loughborough that weekend. And, although they had a number of things planned, they cancelled everything and drove from South Wales to Loughborough.

When Sulwen and Peter arrived they could hear screams. Sulwen was sure it was Tanni screaming but Peter disagreed.

'I'm sure Peter knew it was Tanni,' Sulwen said, 'but, for my sake, he wasn't going to admit it. As we entered, we found them trying to turn Tanni over and she was in excruciating pain.'

From that first moment, Sulwen and Peter were in absolutely no doubt that Tanni needed specialist treatment and that she should immediately be taken back to Cardiff. It was a painful journey with Tanni propped up on pillows and dosed with painkillers.

Peter and Sulwen are still horrified by what they heard of Tanni's treatment in the medical centre. One doctor's knowledge of spina bifida was so scant, he even asked Tanni how she had caught it. This echoed another occasion when a doctor in Cardiff asked Tanni how long she had had the condition!

Exactly how the rod had come out of position is still not clear. Perhaps it was the strain of competing at Seoul, or possibly the result of a fall which Tanni had sustained during training. The winter before, when climbing a rope, Tanni had pulled a muscle under her rib cage and had fallen six or seven feet to the floor. It might have been this which triggered the damage. On reflection, Tanni also feels that her decision to try scuba diving had not helped. The weight of the air tank on her back had caused problems and she recalls feeling a pain in her lower back after a dive. Although the pain went after half an hour of lying on the floor, she fears this incident could have exacerbated the problem.

'What happened during the lecture,' Tanni now believes, 'is that the rod, which had already come out and remained close to my spine, finally came away from it.'

But at that time, the end of 1988, the cause was in some ways immaterial. The treatment and relieving Tanni of the pain were more important. In Cardiff Tanni's back was X-rayed and the investigation showed a huge wall of pus in and around her spine. An emergency operation was immediately decided upon and the minimum dose of antibiotics, prescribed by the Loughborough medical centre, were immediately stepped up to maximum.

'All I can remember about the rod being taken out is that I had a drip in my left hand. It's little niggling things like that which stand out in my mind,' says Tanni recalling her time in hospital. 'One forgets the pain and everything else but remembers the annoyance of having a drip and demanding that it should come out.'

'For a while,' she added, 'they gave some really good pain-killers, including morphine, and I felt fine. I remember timing the hours between the injections and looking forward to the next shot.'

Tanni recovered relatively quickly from the immediate effects of the operation, but knew she had a long period of recovery ahead and began to worry that she was missing too much of the syllabus at Loughborough. Together with the Seoul Games, she missed eight weeks of the first term of the second year and five-and-a-half weeks of the second term. As she grew stronger she was eager to return, even though home is where she normally wants to be nursed and cosseted when she is ill.

She discussed the options. Should she try to continue with her year and risk failing? Could she be set essays to write from a distance? In the end, she opted to return to Loughborough to train and study for the remainder of 1988, and then rejoin her second-year course in the autumn of 1989. This meant that she would be living away from home again and would need to be independent. Her mother would not be able to bring her breakfast and she would have to get up at 7.30 am and go over to the refectory.

'I wanted to be back at Loughborough with my friends and not be sitting at home like a vegetable, doing nothing.'

Peter and Sulwen could see the sense in this. They had been keen initially that she should receive treatment in Cardiff, not only because they felt that this was the best treatment available, but because they could see Tanni every day.

Once in hospital, Tanni wanted to get things over and done with as quickly as possible. Given the option of having the operation to remove the rod after Christmas so that she could spend the festivities at home, she turned this down saying she would rather have the surgery done immediately. In the event the operation was completed in time for Tanni to return home for Christmas. Sian, who was now working as a nurse, was given the job of checking the wound and changing dressings when required. Tanni came out of hospital on Christmas Eve. At that time she was planning to return to university in January, but it quickly became apparent that recovery would take a little longer.

'She was weaker than she thought,' Sulwen remembers. 'Out and about one day, she said "Mum can you push me?" I knew that if she was asking to be pushed, she must be feeling as weak as a kitten.'

In her mind, Tanni knew she would get back to fitness but following her health crisis she was sleeping for up to fifteen hours a day and also knew that training would be completely out of the question for a long time.

By March 1989 however Tanni's strength was returning. She began gentle training and by the summer was back into her old routine. Her first sporting event turned out not to be a wheelchair race but something very different. In May she was roped in to swell the numbers at the World's Biggest Cricket Match organized by Loughborough Students Union.

By early June she was back in her chair racing in earnest, even if somewhat untrained and under-rehearsed. At the 42nd National Wheelchair Games at the Guttmann Sports Centre at Stoke Mandeville, she was one of over 400 athletes from the United Kingdom to take part. Despite her six months of enforced rest from competition, Tanni nevertheless dominated her events. It was an excellent boost to her morale but, since the competition was weak, not much evidence of her return to peak form.

Returning to track fitness also involved remaining up to date with the latest racing wheelchairs. Technology was advancing rapidly and after the Seoul Paralympics the regulations governing the design of racing chairs were changed, resulting in a front steering wheel being added. At Seoul, the rule that chairs should not to be equipped with steering mechanisms because this was too dangerous, was still in force. At this time the chairs had loose front wheels so that, when going into a bend, the athletes could change direction by giving more of a push to one wheel than to the other.

In the view of Tanni and the other athletes this was a crazy arrangement, especially as the speeds that could be achieved were two or three times higher than anything possible in an ordinary day chair. Whereas when Tanni started out as a junior, she might have been able to achieve a speed of ten miles per hour, marathon speeds of twenty-five to thirty miles per hour on downhill stretches were now not unknown. And one of Tanni's rivals, Rose Hill, who trains on the straight roads of Milton Keynes was overtaking the traffic!

Tanni's new chair came by courtesy of a Loughborough company, Beacon Bingo. This company and its patrons, at the instigation of the sub-warden of the Towers on Loughborough campus, raised the cash for Tanni to buy a tailor-made chair.

Accepting the money, raised through the generosity of the bingo players however put Tanni on the spot.

'I was not keen,' she said, 'on being treated as "poor, little, crippled Tanni", but I needed a chair. These days I can usually avoid this approach, but things were different then. The money from Beacon Bingo really helped to push me on a stage. It got me ready for the World Championships in 1990 and I couldn't have done it without them. I don't want to sound ungrateful or cynical but I have changed and times have changed. There are now more people who are willing to think in terms of sponsorship deals rather than charity for disabled people. They are able to appreciate the difference between the two.

'Even now I realize that if I portrayed myself as the poor little cripple I would raise an awful lot more money than I am getting through sponsorship but I prefer to portray myself as an athlete, and I am much more comfortable receiving money that is not given as charity.'

One explanation for Tanni's attitude is not that she is embarrassed or feels demeaned by receiving charity, though she would smart if she felt that she was being patronized. It is because Tanni wonders if she is being dishonest.

'It comes back to people thinking I have a dreadful life because I'm in a wheelchair. People think that disability is so sad, yet here am I jetting around the world, not having to work a conventional nine-to-five routine and doing what I love doing. It's not a sad life at all.'

The new chair that Tanni bought came from the Loughborough-based firm, Bromakin, and she was presented with it, along with a bottle of Champagne, at a ceremony with the Mayor and Mayoress of Charnwood.

Bromakin had been set up by Peter Carruthers, himself a leading wheelchair-racer. He won a Gold in the 100 metres at Seoul, and his interest in manufacturing chairs began when he set out to make a chair for himself. He called on the advice of a bicycle maker, designed a frame and seat, found it worked well and saw the potential of manufacturing chairs for other athletes.

Today, although there are five or six major manufacturers of wheelchairs, the chairs themselves are essentially the same. Before any track event, the competitor needs to adjust the steering to match the precise curvature of the track. This means that when the athlete enters a bend, a small knock on the steering device moves the front wheel to a pre-arranged setting. Once round the bend on the straight, another move of the front wheel brings the chair back into line.

'There's a spring bar,' Tanni explains, 'which attaches from the frame to the fork of the front wheel and a spring-loaded bar with a compensator. There is a V-bar which attaches on to the compensator and the frame and when you come to the bend you knock the V-bar which adjusts the camber and takes the front wheel round. You have to set it at a precise angle with a screw. This only involves the front wheel moving about half a centimetre and that's enough to get round a bend. To steer like this simply means lifting one hand off the wheel for a split second.

'To steer in the old days you had to push with one arm more than the other, which is why learning the new technique took a bit of time. The new tactics mean that there is a lot more pack-racing like cyclists and it isn't only the strongest athlete that wins. The sport is a lot safer and faster and looks better because we have moved away from chairs that resembled horrible little cripple chairs and now have really good equipment.'

The contrast between the new and old generations of racing chairs was summarised by Mary Carol Peterson in the American magazine *Florida Sports*:

> *The technology behind today's racing wheelchairs is spaceshuttle-like stuff. Titanium, carbon fibre and high tech aluminium*

dominate the scene. The racing chair has gone from heavy unwieldy clunker to a sleek sport-specific performance chair.

The article went on to review the history of the wheelchair, going back to the days when racers struggled to compete in steel wheelchairs which weighed 45-55 lb. The cumbersome chairs had to have high backs and push handles measuring 36 inches from the ground, regardless of the height of the occupant. Footplates were also a compulsory feature, although many contestants had no feet. To propel themselves forward, racers had to clumsily reach down to make contact with the push-rim. The two front casters had no steering attached to them while the short wheelbase, in addition to the height at which the racers sat, made hills and corners very dangerous.

Believing it to be fairest for everyone, the NWAA resisted any attempts to modify the standard wheelchair structure to fit individual differences. Only in the 1970s, when an increasing number of athletes became involved with the sport and clamoured for changes, were modifications allowed. Athletes began experimenting with their chairs in order to maximize performance and safety whilst the NWAA continued to revise its requirements to meet with changing technology.

The old steel chairs have now been replaced by a racing machine weighing from 14 to 16 lb with an overall length of 66 inches. A small wheel in the front with two large chambered wheels at the rear, adds the benefits of aerodynamics as well as greater control, speed and stability.

Florida Sports described the state of today's racing wheelchairs:

Bicycle technology has influenced the evolution of the racing chair completely, from calliper brakes to headsets and carbon fibre aerodynamic wheels.

Traditional chair positioning for a wheelchair racer has their knees high and bottoms low. They strap their feet well out of harm's way for safety and aerodynamics. The kneeling position is an option for athletes with trunk control. This position is desirable as the athlete is centred more favourably over the wheel for a more powerful push. The downside of this position is that it is sometimes more difficult to climb hills.

Most successful athletes sit on a lightweight cushion and pay attention to their skin. They know how important it is to maintain healthy skin in their active lifestyles. When trying a new chair, it's recommended that the athlete limits the time in the chair and check their skin for potential problem areas. The chair should sit snugly so that it moves with the athlete, much like a pair of running shoes. It's important to be measured by a knowledgeable professional.

Despite all the technological advances, a race is still a gruelling event and Tanni's toughest race of the year was the British Wheelchair Marathon held at Porthcawl, South Wales in September.

The race started in appalling weather with strong winds and lashing rain but the harsh conditions eased as the race went on. In was an open event without classification and men and women competed together. Tanni was up against Chris Hallam, who even though sustaining a puncture within the first half mile, managed to make up a deficit of over five minutes and win the race in 2 hours 21 minutes. Tanni in a tight race to the finish with Chris Baggley came joint thirteenth in 3 hours 4 seconds. If Tanni needed anything to prove her fitness, that race with a sprint finish in demanding weather fitted the bill.

By this time however Tanni's mind was turning to warmer weather and greater challenges. The Commonwealth Games, to be held in New Zealand in January 1990, was planning to include two demonstration wheelchair races, an 800 metres for women and a 1500 metres for men.

Initially the New Zealand Paralympic and Physically Disabled Federation, which was arranging the event, did not invite Wales to submit any entries, despite Wales having in Chris Hallam and Tanni Grey two outstanding Paralympians. However, by January invitations had been received and both Chris and Tanni were making arrangements to travel to the Antipodes. Tanni flew out of London on the 26 January. Chris was already down under and met up with Tanni in New Zealand.

Tanni's parents were somewhat alarmed that Tanni had no firm idea who would be meeting her at the other end.

'I would have wanted everything dotted and crossed,' Sulwen says. 'But Tanni just said, well somebody will meet me and know who I am because I'll be in a wheelchair.'

The Commonwealth Games, although obviously not of Olympian status, are nevertheless international games of the very highest quality. They are truly cosmopolitan as, thanks to the history of the British Empire, the Commonwealth includes members from almost every continent. Britain does not compete as a nation, but national teams are sent from each of the nations which make up the United Kingdom.

As a host city, Tanni found Auckland a far cry from Seoul. Everything was so familiar, she could almost have been in Britain. On her arrival she penned a quick postcard home.

> *Well I got here – finally! We had to do a complete change in LA so I did get to see it (well the airport lounge).*
>
> *Auckland is beautiful. Been to see a bit of it already. Having a bit of hassle getting passes to see the track but hopefully that will change. Anyway take care, I'll see you soon, Love Tan.*

Although her event was not of full medal status and was meant to be a demonstration of a new sport, Tanni was still able to savour the full atmosphere of an athletics' meeting which was not solely for disabled sportsmen and women. She was, in her own right, one of a team of the elite from her home country. She finished third behind the two Canadians in a time of 2 minutes 27 seconds, an improvement of 15 seconds on her previous best. If medals had been awarded she would have received a Bronze.

'I was very pleased with the race, especially as right up until the start there was lots of politics and there seemed to be some doubt about whether the exhibition race would be allowed to go ahead.'

Chris Hallam describes how, as disabled athletes, they were not able to take a full part in the Games. They were not allowed to live in the 'plush quarters' reserved for able-bodied athletes.

'We stayed in some shabby school in the middle of nowhere. My first experience of competing at a top able-bodied event was that we were treated as less than equal.'

Tanni certainly confirms his recollections. Between them, they could only find one Welsh vest to compete in and somehow Chris's muscular torso had to be squeezed into Tanni's racing top.

'I suppose, at that time, disabled sport was only just starting to get on the map and the Welsh team didn't give us any recognition or an awful lot of help.'

The trip was not funded from the same sources as the able-bodied team. It was paid for by the British Wheelchair Sports Foundation at Stoke Mandeville.

Tanni was not the only Loughborough University athlete to produce a personal best at the Games. Achieving a Common-wealth record of 86.90 metres, Steve Backley took the Gold in the javelin.

The year after an Olympic or Paralympic Games is normally a quiet one for athletes, but by 1990 in addition to the Commonwealth Games, Tanni was back at Loughborough racing in the Loughborough 10 km road race and the Midland Banks National Student Games. She also had a number of her own records in her sights.

Up until then Tanni had made her name as a sprinter, but after a successful 10 km road race at Loughborough in April 1990 in which she recorded a new personal best of 32 minutes 51 seconds, she began to feel optimistic about tackling even longer distances. She had already applied to take part in the London Marathon two weeks later and had concentrated her training programme on building up her stamina and speed.

In Tanni's view, the London Marathon is a very important event because it is one of the few major national events which shows wheelchairs on television and is almost the only occasion, aside from the Paralympics, when wheelchair racing is on full view as a spectator sport.

'It is not just the odd second that is shown of a poor disabled person struggling, they show the elite disabled people at the front and the level of competition between them. This is very important from the point of view of motivating other people with disabilities to actually go out and take part. I don't really like the expression 'role model' but without actually seeing people like me doing the marathon many people with disabilities wouldn't go out and take part. It helps in the slow process of changing able-bodied people's attitudes towards disability.

'It is the wheelchair racers who cross the line ahead of the fastest runners. And as the whole marathon is televised from start to finish the wheelchair athletes get their fair share of publicity.'

The code of conduct for wheelchair competitors in mass running events brought home to Tanni that a wheelchair is a potential hazard to a competitor on foot, and one collision could lead to serious and permanent injury. The officials gave her a whole range of rules and regulations to digest, and told her that all clacksons and warning devices were banned on chairs, and that, for safety reasons, she should carry her own liquid refreshment and avoid using the drinking stations.

The atmosphere at the start of a London Marathon is unique. Thousands of runners mill around shivering in the cold ready for their big challenge, doing gentle muscle-easing exercises or, in the case of people like Tanni, suffering from nerves and throwing up – something which Tanni experiences before every major race. She describes the build up like this:

'I don't sleep very well the night before and wake up feeling like death warmed up. I then tend to feel worse and worse until ten minutes before the marathon when I get so nervous I vomit. But that's quite normal for me. If I'm not feeling sick and not actually being sick, I think there's something wrong. Perhaps I'm even at the stage when I actually make myself sick before a race because it has become my way of coping with the nerves. It's just part of the racing.'

Some of the London Marathon participants are novice racers, some are so experienced that they carry their own stop-watches and are disappointed if they do not finish within the top fifty.

Lining up with Tanni were many familiar faces and many fellow competitors she was to get to know very well. It was not Tanni's first marathon. She had recorded a previous best of 3 hours 4 minutes and as a teenager she had been taken on a half-marathon, pushed by runner Frank Trott, which had lasted 2 hours 18 minutes. This however was her first time under the spotlight of the London Marathon.

When she crossed the line at Westminster, having covered the 26-plus miles from Greenwich, Tanni had taken 15 minutes off her personal best. This might have been 22 minutes had she not at 21 miles suffered a puncture and lost 7 minutes. Chas Saddler and John Harris stopped to fix the tyre with her.

'On my day chair,' she said, 'I have solid tyres which go anywhere and of course don't puncture. On the racing chair I put new tyres on for big races and keep a spare set with me that I train on. I keep a good eye on them but, in the end, it is just bad luck if a wheel goes during a race.'

Tanni was just four minutes outside the British record and came in fourth. Connie Hansen was first and the best British competitor was Rose Hill who came in third. Taking the honours that year in the men's running race was the first British man to win the London Marathon for five years, a thirty-five year old Scot named Allister Hutton. The women's race was won by runner Wanda Panfil. Chris Hallam was the first Britain home in the wheelchair race but, having won the marathon twice, he was beaten this time by overseas competition. Swede Hackan Ericsson finished the men's wheelchair race in 1 hour 57 minutes 12 seconds and Connie Hansen of Denmark won the women's race in 2 hours 10 minutes 25 seconds.

Despite the unpleasant weather, with wind and rain all the way, Tanni finished thirtieth in the wheelchair field of sixty men and women. She beat a number of leading men and was involved in a tight finish with Rose Hill who beat her by just eight seconds.

Runners talk of 'hitting the wall' during the marathon. This is the point when physical exhaustion and pain almost overwhelms them and the greatest determination is needed if they are to continue. Wheelchair marathon racers do not normally hit the wall in the same way because, although they get as tired as any other elite athlete, they do not have to carry their body weight around the course and propel it in the same way as a runner. On downhill stretches the effort also eases. It is also possible in a wheelchair to let the front runner take the brunt of the wind resistance and draft along behind them.

After her first London Marathon, Tanni recalls experiencing utter exhaustion. The final metres needed a tremendous effort of will and, while she was mending her puncture, her body cooled down so much that when she started going again, working particularly hard over the last quarter of the race to catch up, the agony she experienced was unlike anything she had ever felt before.

'It was really awful. I had blurred vision, was sick and felt absolutely dreadful. Then, as I do after every London Marathon I said I'm never going to do it again. I hate it. But then by the time the entry forms comes round the next year I forget all the nasty bits and just remember the good bits.'

Following the marathon, Tanni had a diary full of competitive engagements, peaking in July when she was invited by the British Paraplegic Sports Society to join the British team for the World Championships in track athletics in Assen, the Netherlands.

Before that, Tanni's engagements included a 1500 metres wheelchair duel at the Cardiff Athletics Stadium. It was a battle of the sexes between the Paralympic pentathlete, John Harris, from Cwmbran and Tanni.

They were very closely matched and both shared the lead at different stages of the race. Tanni finally clinched victory with a spurt during the final metres. Her time was 4 minutes 48.13 seconds. The duel was part of a special afternoon of athletics arranged for sportsmen and women of all ages with a variety of disabilities.

Winning in fact became a common feature of Tanni's 1990 season. At the British Wheelchair Racing Association track championships at Birmingham on the 12 May, she won the 100, 200, 400, 800, 1500 and 5000 metres events. And at the National Wheelchair Games at Stoke Mandeville in June, having taken four Gold medals in the 100, 200, 400 and 800 metres, she was awarded the Bryn Davis trophy as the most improved athlete. In June that year, she also held the British track records at seven distances, despite the fact that in terms of classification her disability was considered to be more severe than that of many of her key rivals.

Interestingly, five of the longer distance track records were set in 1990 whilst Tanni did not improve on her 100 and 200 metres times, recorded respectively at Seoul in 1988 and Switzerland in 1989.

A quick comparison between her BWRA track championship certificate of participation of 1989 with that of 1990 makes the point clearly: in 1990 in the 100 metres Tanni, while winning on both occasions, was 0.4 seconds slower than she had been the year before. In the 200 metres her time again was slower, this time by the very narrowest of margins 0.1 seconds. However her 400 metres time had improved by 4 seconds, her 800 metres performance by 5 seconds and her 1500 metres time by 31 seconds.

In many ways, the inauguration of the World Championships and Games for the Disabled mirrored the cycle of the Olympiad. It was the opportunity for all the elite athletes of the world to compete together outside an Olympic year.

Travelling to Holland was not, perhaps, as exciting as a trip to Seoul or New Zealand, so Tanni had few diversions. In her usual way on arrival, she sent a couple of chirpy postcards to her parents, writing:

Well, here's a card from Holland, what can I say? I've seen no tulips, few dogs and tons of bikes. Weather is good, food is fine, accommodation is average. See you all before you get this.

106

And to Sian, she wrote:

> *Piggy – some clogs from Holland, how original. How's life, I've nearly got sun stroke. Anyway Piglet back to the tiring life of being an international track athlete. Love Tan.*

At the spectacular opening ceremony an audience of 22,000 people applauded Princess Margriet as she declared the Games open in front of the 3500 competitors who were lined up.

Up against international competition, Tanni found the going tough but improved on her performance at Seoul by taking Silver medals in the 100 and 200 metres as well as a Bronze in the 400 metres. These contributed to a British total of 41 Gold, 37 Silver and 20 Bronze medals. Once again Germany and the United States led the medal table.

With the exception of a mention on BBC television's *Grandstand*, the Games received little publicity. The British press was far more interested in the World Wheelchair Games at Stoke Mandeville which followed. Was this because the controversial Fergie, Duchess of York was scheduled to open them? At the time there were fears that she would not arrive because she might need to make a trip to Argentina to visit her stepfather who was seriously ill. In the event, she arrived by helicopter wearing a bright green floral silk dress and spent an hour chatting to competitors, including Tanni.

In her opening speech the Duchess of York said:

'Today no one can be in any doubt about the physical, psychological and social effects sport, whether leisure or competition, has on the life of a disabled person'.

She also quoted Sir Ludwig Guttmann's words to the disabled: 'It is not what you have lost but what you have left that counts'.

The Games confirmed Tanni's growing strength as a long-distance competitor and once again suggested that her performances as a sprint athlete had reached a plateau. She took medals in the 100 and 800 metres track events, but the high spot of the Games for her was winning the women's open marathon, beating Ingrid Lauridsen with a new personal best and achieving a British record time of 2 hours 20 minutes 25 seconds.

In *Replay*, the daily news-sheet of the Games, she was asked how she managed to train for sprints as well as middle- and long-distance events. She explained that, across the board, the same theories of work applied. As a wheelchair athlete, she did not use her weight-bearing muscles and this meant she could anticipate being able to compete at a top level for many years without needing to change from sprint to longer distances as runners often had to do.

However, it should be pointed out that in coming third in the 100 metres, Tanni earned a new British record and her own personal best, breaking the 20 seconds barrier for the first time at 19.14 seconds. The fact that this only earned her a Bronze medal showed how far and how fast women wheelchair-racers were improving. Tanni was also one of the youngest participants and her winning time, plus the knowledge that she had a number of seasons in hand to improve, raised her hopes for the Paralympic Games.

Following the Games, Tanni took part in the television programme *We are the Champions* disabled special from the National Sports Centre for Wales. The presenter was Ron Pickering and the programme involved both demonstrations and celebrations of disability sport.

'I think we're proving,' Tanni said on air, 'if you didn't know it already, that being disabled does not mean you can't take part in sport. In fact, there's no limit to the sports disabled people can take up – even if you're in a wheelchair you can still go sailing, canoeing, or even hanging upside down off a cliff.'

Tanni saw her involvement in *We are the Champions* as an opportunity to encourage children with disabilities to become involved in disabled sport. But she was also only too aware that, in doing this on screen, she was walking a tightrope. Inevitably, many people watching the programme would see the children with a patronizing eye. Certainly the attitudes of some of the television crew left much to be desired. It was not that they meant to be patronizing, quite the opposite, but their approach to disabled people came across as over-sympathetic and patronising.

In his letter thanking Tanni for taking part in the programme, the producer, Peter Charlton, referred to the behaviour of one of the broadcast team. He 'did a bit of head-patting from time to time. Sorry about that; his heart is in the right place but he hasn't had that much experience of working with disabled adults. I hope you weren't too annoyed!'

Later on, in September, Tanni was able to encourage potential junior athletes on her own terms when she was invited to be guest of honour and open the National Junior Wheelchair Games arranged by the British Paraplegic Sports Society. There she was introduced as *The Times*'s Student Sportswoman of the Year and holder of four world records.

Four days later Tanni was racing again, but not solely, this time, to promote a cause but as a sportswoman on the circuit. It was the day of the Great North Run from Newcastle to South Shields. She took the half-marathon race in 1 hour 6 minutes, earning herself £600 and a watch as prize. There was an additional satisfaction, too. She had defeated Rose Hill who, that summer, had been her main British rival, taking from her the British track records at Stoke Mandeville in the 5,000 and 10,000 metres events.

What made the competition even fiercer between Tanni and Rose Hill was that they were competing head-on in the British Wheelchair Racing Association Grand Prix series. When they arrived in Dublin for the final marathon of the season they both knew that one slip would cost either of them the title. By that time the men's event had already been decided, with Chris Hallam taking the £700 winner's cheque with a maximum of 90 points but in the women's event things could not have been closer.

It was a good day for Tanni. The conditions were right and she finished the marathon course in 2 hours 18 minutes 4 seconds, two minutes ahead of Rose and the Grand Prix title was shared. Her time was a massive improvement on her pre-season best. The prize-winning ceremony was held at Stoke Mandeville on 17 November, sponsored by the chair makers Bromakin, whose founder Peter Carruthers incidentally won the quadriplegic class.

Tanni's new time meant that she was not only some 30 minutes faster than Yvonne Holloway, the fifth fastest wheelchair woman marathon racer in Britain, but only 13 minutes behind the top ten men. Having only two years before been seen as a specialist sprinter, Tanni had now achieved success in a gruelling season of marathons and half-marathons.

That summer she raced in some appalling weather conditions, the worst being at Sleaford in the half-marathon at the end of September. Here, as she and Rose raced to the line, so close that barely a second separated them, her time of 1 hour 13 minutes and 8 seconds was the same as that of the third placed man, Barry Cooper. This was an open-class race with no allowance being made for Tanni's classification. Tanni's time was so improved that at Dublin, where the Grand Prix title was clinched, she would have taken a Bronze if she had raced in the men's event!

By the end of the year invitations were coming in not so much to Tanni the competitor, but Tanni the personality. She was asked on to the *Sports Review of the Year* programme for 1990, broadcast on 16 December by BBC Television.

To give the impression that life for a full-time athlete, such as Tanni, is just a matter of going from competition to competition and gala event to gala event, would be misleading. The real work involves a hard daily grind of training which has to be done with iron self-discipline and determination in all conditions, whether the body feels like it or not.

Tanni's training programme consists of weight-lifting and road work and specialist speed trials at a stadium. She builds up stamina covering long distances in her sports chair around the streets of Cardiff and the track of the Athletics Stadium. Her training is not a matter of following a haphazard routine, but is carefully worked out with the help of her coach to maximize her potential and allow for her prowess to peak on the right occasions at the right events. The work is hard on her body, and particularly hard on her hands which have to be carefully gloved to protect them from the cuts, grazes and bruises which result from steadily pushing and rhythmically moving the wheels of the sporting chair.

Today Tanni relies on two people for help – Dave Williams in Cardiff who used to coach the Welsh Men's Athletic Team and Jenny Banks, a former hockey international player and now one of the world's foremost coaches of disabled athletes who works for the Australian Paralympic Association. Tanni phones her regularly in Sydney, Australia, time-difference permitting, and teams up with her in Australia whenever she can. Training tasks and goals are set. Dave is on hand in Wales for the track sessions, and Jenni and Tanni communicate by fax and telephone. The quarterly bill for Tanni's use of her BT line is substantial.

At present, Tanni is working on a four-week cycle with two weeks building up to a third week of hard work and a fourth easier week which she spends in recovering. Monday through to Saturday consists of pre-programmed training sessions – only Sunday is a day off. As with any track athlete a top performance is a matter of isolating the various elements, concentrating on them, and then putting them together like building blocks at the end to make a final performance.

Tanni concentrates on starts, which for her are a weaker area, and then sets about improving the way she picks up speed and gathers a rhythm. She also has to concentrate on her stamina and must always be thinking about tactics. A 17-second sprint over 100 metres is largely an anaerobic surge of activity. Anything over that involves the use of the aerobic capacity of the body and requires maximum use of the lungs and heart.

One advantage of having a variety of things to concentrate upon is that it relieves some of the boredom of constant training. Tanni sees herself primarily as a short-distance athlete, even though she has done well at distance up to marathon. She plans her training at least a year in advance, especially if there is a major event ahead. All her 1995/96 training programme, for instance, has been aimed at Atlanta.

Training is not always a lone pursuit. Sian may accompany Tanni on a bicycle as she spins around the roads of Cardiff.

'It depends on what shifts I am working at the hospital,' Sian says, 'and what the weather conditions are like.'

'It helps me,' her sister observes, 'because Sian can pace me along in certain sessions and it's just nice having company. I'm not competitive with Sian.'

On the track, runner Andrew Webber teams up with Tanni because they find their training programmes complement each other. Andrew, who is a Welsh internationalist and specialist in 400 metres, came to know Tanni through Dave Williams. When two athletes can push each other along in training it is to their mutual advantage. For Tanni, knowing that Andrew is just ahead or behind gives her an extra 3 miles per hour of speed.

'This arrangement helps me as much as it does her,' Andrew says. 'I know when she's behind me because I can hear her. I then press on with something to aim for. It really works very well for both of us. I've also borrowed Sian's mountain bike and gone out with Tanni on some of her longer distances. At the end, she finds that because of me she's been significantly quicker than she would have been if she'd been training by herself. This is simply because of that extra psychological spur you get knowing that there's someone pushing you along.'

This arrangement however has not been without its hazards and Tanni recalls a couple of times when she has over-steered!

'I remember when my steering was rather loose and made things a little unpredictable around the bends but fortunately we never had a major collision and now we are very used to training with each other.'

Away from the track, in the gymnasium, Dave Williams advises her on several aspects her training and is also the one who keeps her on the straight and narrow and bullies her when her usual determination and self-discipline flag.

'He nags me about the coffee I drink,' Tanni admits. 'But as far as my training is concerned he doesn't have to nag. He's more of an adviser than a coach. We talk about what's coming up, what I need to do to peak and what I want to peak for. Then he oversees the training plans. He then advises me about whether or not the programme is going in the right direction, about the way I am pushing, and comes up with ideas that I might not have thought of. It's good to have someone looking over my shoulder.

'I do weight-training two or three times a week – I find it hard and boring and don't really like it. It's just something I have to do throughout the winter to get strong enough for competitions in the summer season. I might look frail but I'm tough because I've been training so hard for so long. I always have to be aware of possible damage to my spine. As someone with spina bifida, I also have to have regular medical check-ups to make sure that I am not developing other problems with the kidneys. I try to make sure I do the right thing so I will not harm myself for the future. I'm fairly sure I'm going to have problems with my hands and shoulders later on in life and I've accepted that. It's just part of being an athlete. But with things like kidney damage which could be serious, I have to be particularly careful not to damage myself.

'Training in all disciplines is painful because the pain is not outweighed by the potential triumph of a race.'

Tanni also trains with fellow wheelchair athlete, Ian Thompson, whom she first met in 1986 on a training weekend. Today she is a frequent visitor to his home at Redcar and, when there, they always share joint training sessions. However, because Ian is much faster than Tanni, she does not, she says, find training with him as helpful as it might be.

'There's always an element of competition between us and when he's training flat out, I can't keep up. On the other hand, if he slows down for me he's not working hard enough himself.'

Ian Thompson took a PhD in chemistry and at thirty-one is six years older than Tanni. Prior to 2 October 1984 he was a keen competitive cyclist, but in a split second on that day his concentration lapsed and he and his bicycle collided with a bus. He can now walk with a stick, but needs a wheelchair for any distance. He took up wheelchair-racing in 1986 and sees similarities between the sport and cycling.

113

When his path first crossed with Tanni's, she recalls finding him obnoxious and remembers him, having just commenced on his post-graduate research, making a derogatory comment about the 'PE college' where she was an undergraduate.

Since then however Tanni has discovered his better qualities and he and Tanni spend a great deal of time in each other's company. 'She didn't quite understand my sense of humour at first,' Ian says of Tanni's first reaction to him.

They are both much involved as competitors although Ian, who is an industrial chemist researching into synthetic lubricants, is not a full-time athlete. They both have leading roles in the wheelchair racing organization, the British Wheelchair Racing Association.

When training, Tanni has to be careful not to push herself one hundred per cent all the time. She knows that pacing herself is a necessary precaution.

Would Tanni push herself as hard as she does if she were not winning, if she were just mediocre at her event? She claims not to be able to answer that question. She carries on, she says, because she likes winning but she also accepts that when she is older she will start to go downhill physically and that deciding when to stop will be very difficult. Fellow track athlete Tracey Lewis now believes that her own health problems, which kept her away from top competition between the Barcelona and Atlanta games, came about because she pushed herself too hard when training.

For Tanni, the next logical development from training with an able-bodied runner is to compete against able-bodied athletes. She sees no reason why wheelchair-racing should not be an entirely open event.

'The wheelchair,' she says, 'is a device, just like a bicycle, and it enables a disabled athlete to compete on equal terms with someone who is able-bodied.'

Andrew Webber would certainly be interested in having a go. He has never tried Tanni's chair because it is too small for him but, should one of the elite men be around with a chair that would fit him, he would love to give it a try.

'More than anything else,' he said, 'I would like to see what it is like to travel that fast without using my legs.'

The idea of wheelchair-racing being an open event is a controversial one. There are already a handful of able-bodied wheelchair-racers, but many spectators think that, given these competitors can walk, this is cheating.

One of the country's most active wheelchair-racers is Chas Saddler, and his able-bodied son has shown considerable interest in the sport. He has borrowed his father's chair, practised in it with other athletes, and has even entered races. As a result of this interest and enthusiasm, he has been on the receiving end of some very carping publicity. Nevertheless, Tanni sees wheelchair-racing as an open event that potentially has a great future and she hopes that one day it will be given full Olympic status.

When two athletes, even those in different disciplines, train together they often have more to offer each other than specialist advice relating to sport. Andrew is not as successful as Tanni, he still needs to earn a living as a civil servant and cannot turn full-time professional, but when he is injured or feeling a bit down it is useful, he finds, to have Tanni around to moan to.

'There have been numerous occasions, too many to mention, when she's had to listen to me,' he says. 'For example, when I had to change jobs or had a bust up with an old girlfriend, she listened to all my complaints. She has a good ear.'

There is also much banter and humour around, especially when Sian joins them.

As well as track, the Cyncoed College gymnasium and the stadium, there is one other place where Tanni can train. She has in the past kept a set of static rollers in the dining room of her house and can train at great speed without moving any distance.

It is an extremely boring way of covering no distance at all, just staring at a wall or a cupboard, even though that cupboard holds an array of the cups and medals she has won. That form of training is a last resort when the weather is too foul to do otherwise.

115

While Andrew and Tanni work together well on the athletics track, in terms of status in the sporting world they are a long way apart. Tanni once invited Andrew to accompany her to a formal dinner and presentation to which she had been invited as a guest of honour. He remembers sitting there in his best clothes alongside sporting heroes and television personalities and being given the full red-carpet treatment because he was Tanni's guest. He also remembers how unfazed by it all Tanni was.

'There she was stuffing her face with food and there was I thinking what on earth am I doing in this company? It's second nature to her but, to me, it was all an amazing surprise. She handles it so well and takes everything in her stride.'

The winter of 1991 was one again a winter of hard work, in all weathers, to maintain speed and stamina in her events. While the rewards for athletes who have not reached the top might be few for all this effort, the invitations to Tanni to attend prestige events kept rolling in.

On the 27 February 1991 she attended the British Sports Association for the Disabled Media Awards, in the ballroom of the Carlton Tower Hotel. Tanni was there to represent the sport as the Princess of Wales presented the awards to the top journalists, television programme-makers and radio producers who had made the greatest contribution to reporting on disability sport. A delightful photograph was taken of Tanni watching Rachael, daughter of Frank Bruno, presenting a bouquet to Princess Diana.

A few days before a letter had been sent, by the organizers of the event, containing what was described as some useful tips for the day. They amounted to what to do when meeting royalty!

The letter advised Tanni that a member of the royal family always starts the conversation and that she must wait to be spoken to. She was also told that, in conversation, she should say 'Your Royal Highness' on the first occasion she addressed the Princess and after that 'Ma'am' ('as in jam' the letter hinted!) The instruction that amused Tanni most was the one that said that a bow from a gentleman and a curtsy from a lady is expected when presented to Her Royal Highness. No instructions were given as to how a lady was expected to curtsy in a wheelchair.

The glamour of the occasion might have led observers to conclude that disability sport has no problems in raising money from sponsorship. But by April there were serious worries that a number of the important summer events might have to be cancelled because sponsorship money was not available. They were not events that would directly affect Tanni, being table tennis, bowls and junior athletics but it was a sign that the less glamorous activities were not attracting the funding they should.

In the spring of 1991, despite all her reservations and best intentions, Tanni was again entered for the London Marathon. The air was a little chilled but the sky was blue and clear when the runners set out. They took the course from Greenwich, round by the Thames barrier to the Cutty Sark, along through the Surrey Docks and Rotherhithe to Tower Bridge. Then, after a journey through Docklands and the City, they came to the home straight along the Embankment via Buckingham Palace to the finish at Westminster Bridge.

Twenty-five thousand runners took to the road with two reigning Olympic champions to the forefront. Chris Hallam was again the British favourite and Connie Hansen, of Denmark, was tipped for the women's event with rivals Ericsson, Lindkvist and Holding all seeded.

In the pre-race coverage of the event Jane Wyatt of *The Times* helped feed the growing interest in the event with some additional technical knowledge about it.

'Wheelchair road racing is more akin to cycling than running, with competitors preferring to keep in packs to aid slipstream. There are then surges of speed within the packs to try and wear people down. Shortly before the end the leaders reduce speed in preparation for a final sprint to the line.'

There were also descriptions of the chairs in use, each costing around £1,000 with wheels made from aluminium alloy, tyres inflated up to 130 lb per square inch pressure and the two rear wheels splayed inwards to maximize pushing action. The gloves were also described. In many cases these are wrapped in tape for extra padding.

Some of the chairs, it was reported, carried a sensor picking up information from the back wheel for a computer mounted on the handlebars. This was an important feature for an elite racer like Tanni. The claim was also made that, on one occasion, Chas Saddler been trapped by police radar doing 35 miles per hour on a downhill run.

Then, just as the media was beginning to grasp an understanding of the competition rules, there was controversy behind the scenes following the 1991 Stoke Mandeville marathon. Tanni found herself at the centre of the storm for using what a number of racers claimed was an unfair tactic.

Tanni, believing as she now says that the tactic was legitimate, had drafted behind some of the male competitors to gain advantage from their shelter and speed. This enabled her to go a fraction faster before re-positioning herself and sprinting to the finish.

When Tanni was criticized for using this technique she was defended by race officials, who said that athletes have always used whatever tactics are available to them within the rules. However, it was, they added, a tactic that they would like to see excluded from racing and that ways of outlawing it were being explored.

Tanni says that she had been advised before the event that the tactic would be acceptable, even though some might see it as unsporting. Since the incident, she has not repeated that method. Looking back on the controversy, Tanni says:

'The team decided that possibly Rose Hill and I could be helped round the course by other team mates. At the time I was naive enough to think that, as it was suggested by team mates, it was okay. In the event I dropped Rose at the start of the race and used the tactic. Afterwards I was not particularly proud of the fact that there was a controversy. Although not cheating, it is bending the rules as far as they will go. I have never used the tactic since to beat anyone. I have done it in races where other women are using this tactic, and in some races abroad it is considered acceptable, but never to beat someone the way I did Ingrid. I have a lot of respect for Ingrid as an athlete and feel sorry that I was naive and did it this way.'

The men's London Marathon was later described as a cat-and-mouse affair between the top five men. In the last 200 metres it was the speed of Farid Maarouch, from France, which gained the advantage winning 4 minutes outside the course record in 1 hour 52 minutes 52 seconds.

In the women's race, Connie Hansen did not disappoint and came in 12 minutes behind the leading man; Rose Hill came second, 16 minutes behind Connie; and Tanni Grey 34 minutes behind. Only 10 seconds separated the first five men home and Connie's easy victory was evidence that in the marathon, at that stage, the women's event was not drawing the potential competitors that it might have done.

Looming even larger in Tanni's mind than any of her races was the final stage of her degree course. Having deferred taking this by a year, because of the spine operation, the spring and summer of 1991 was the time of reckoning. Despite all the breaks for sport, all the time spent training, as well as her illness and hospitalization, Tanni gained a second-class degree. On Thursday 11 July she went forward in her black gown and Loughborough purple hood to receive it.

No longer was she to be described in print as 'student Tanni Grey'. Now, with her university life over, she had to decide how to make a living. With her eyes set firmly on Barcelona in 1992, giving up sport was not something she was prepared to contemplate. Her successes and rewards, in all their various forms, were not something she wanted to give up. Indeed giving them up barely entered her mind.

In due course a number of ideas came to her. She looked to studying for a postgraduate degree and the world of public relations also interested her. Although she did not really think of it as a viable option at the time, there was the possibility of earning her keep through working for various promotional causes. This however depended on her maintaining a high profile as an athlete. Prior to Barcelona, to buy time to train and consider options, Peter and Sulwen offered to help out.

Maintaining that high profile on the track in 1991 did not turn out to be a major obstacle for Tanni. At the World Wheelchair Games at Stoke Mandeville, Tanni took the 100 metres Gold. She missed a world record by half a second when winning the 200 metres in 36 seconds and finished second in the women's 400 metres.

At the Games, and throughout 1991, she was able to show that her sprint-racing had not reached a plateau and that her training programme of the winter had enabled her both to compete at a top level in the long-distance events and to improve at the shorter distances.

In 1992 Tanni's work bore fruit and she was able to start the Paralympic year with a win in the prestigious London Marathon. The marathon is not only a very high profile event for wheelchair athletes but one of the world's most demanding marathon courses. Wheelchairs have to cope with the city's ancient streets which can be very jarring for competitors used to modern, smooth road surfaces. It is also held in the spring, at a time of year when the weather is particularly unpredictable. Occasionally, the rain and wind make it appear as if winter has returned.

Tanni's elation at winning made it all seem worth it. 'It was,' she said, 'the perfect way to start the season on which I'd been concentrating my training for so long.'

While an event such as the London Marathon is open to wheelchair-users with all types of disability, the World Wheelchair Games are organized strictly on the lines of classification. As with the Paralympics, at the Wheelchair Games an attempt is made to enable athletes with similar disabilities to compete against each other.

It would be unfair for the winning of a wheelchair race to be determined simply by how little a person is disabled. People whose spinal injuries are low in the back, allowing them maximum torso and shoulder power, would always win over those with higher spinal breaks.

So, for the benefit of competition, wheelchair athletes are divided into four categories. The system now used is a simplified version of the old one that was initially designed only for those who had received spinal injuries in accidents, not for people with spina bifida. Now that each athlete is assessed by a medical panel, the classification can reflect function rather than just the medical condition, and disabled people from various categories might well be classified as able to compete together. At the moment however for wheelchair-racing those with spinal injuries are assessed in a different way from those with disabilities such as cerebral palsy.

In wheelchair sport a T1 is someone with a very high lesion, a quadriplegic who has very little bicep, tricep or forearm power and might not even have movement in the fingers. They would have been injured from the top of the chest down.

A T2 is, again, a quadriplegic but with an injury at a lower level so that there would be some bicep power, but the individual would not have the whole use of their arms or the best co-ordination with their fingers. They would normally be injured from the middle of the chest down.

T3 is for paraplegics who have the full use of their arms but do not have good stomach or back muscles. (Tanni falls within this range.) Those who are T4 have stomach and back muscles and include amputees. Athletes with spina bifida are much in the minority with only few names such as Jean Driscoll, Andy Hodge and Tracey Lewis being recognized at a senior level.

'Classification used to be done purely by medical definition,' Tanni explains. 'But now doctors classify not only on medical grounds but also on the way you push. It's a fairer system as it cracks down on people cheating and getting into the wrong class.'

Is there a danger that a person might, through good training, raise themselves from one classification to another? This would not mean that the spinal severance would alter but that their mode of pushing and their general strength would improve. Tanni does not see this as a problem. She will always, she believes, remain a T3 but acknowledges that as she gets stronger and better the classifiers might look at her again to see if there is any reason why she should not be lifted to the next category.

Tanni believes though that she has been a T3 for so long that if her classification were to be changed it would have happened by now. She is quite philosophical about the situation and if she was moved to the T4 category she would accept it. After all, in the open events, she is already competing against T4s and frequently winning. At present, Tanni explains, T3 and T4 athletes compete up to 800 metres apart because the lack of stomach muscles has a substantial effect on the way in which the athletes start a race.

Compared to T4 athletes, Tanni's start is slower. She cannot keep her body down on her knees and give herself the explosive start that a lot of the athletes in the T4 category have developed. A T4 can hold his or her body much firmer and get away quicker.

Getting a good start is crucial in winning a race up to 800 metres. From 1500 metres onwards the start is not so crucial and T3 and T4 women compete together. In terms of time the differences are not huge. Approximately one second is involved on the 100 metres, 2 seconds on 200 metres, 4 seconds on 400 metres and 6 seconds on 800 metres. Almost all of that relates to the start. In exhibition events, where Tanni competes with T4 athletes, she knows that she will never win. But she is so far ahead of so many in the T3 category that she is able to put in a very respectable performance in the company of the T4s. As she has already done, she can break T3 records competing in a T3/T4 open race and yet not win the race.

Before finishing her time at Loughborough and collecting her degree, Tanni took a very full and energetic part in many student activities. These included the Loughborough rag, an annual event of nonsense justified by its ability to raise large sums of money for good causes. As someone who, ever since she was very young, has found herself on the receiving end of charity and being seen as a good cause in her own right, Tanni has ambivalent attitudes towards money raising.

She is unhesitant in her enthusiasm for voluntary agencies, such as the People's Dispensary for Sick Animals, feeling that no moral issues arise there. However, when it comes to raising money for organizations connected with disability or to help people requiring medical help over and above that which the National Health Service provides, she can see some strength in the arguments put forward by political activists in the disability movement.

The battle cry of 'Rights not Charity', which is often used at demonstrations supporting a civil rights disability bill, is one which strikes a chord with Tanni. Although much good is done through charitable giving, it is perhaps most noticeably the donors who benefit through being able to perform such unselfish acts rather than the recipients, who can frequently feel uneasy.

Tanni nevertheless recognizes that receiving charitable gifts is the only option some people have if they wish to pursue life to the full. Certainly, Tanni's own career as an athlete could not have taken off without the money-raising efforts of voluntary organizations such as the Rotary Club and the generosity of a number of large companies. The fact that some of the companies decided to use their generosity to achieve self-publicity is another matter.

Tanni is also aware that much more money can be raised for charitable use if the person or group for whom the money is intended, are willing to portray themselves as having a substantially diminished quality of life.

'The poor little cripple raises more money than someone who appears fitter and healthier, even though that person might be seriously disabled,' Tanni observes.

By becoming involved in charitable fundraising, Tanni feels she might be perpetuating society's negative attitude towards disability. But does she therefore feel that she should give up money-raising efforts altogether?

'It is a difficult decision.' she says, 'A dilemma – I drift between both points of view. I would certainly rather not raise money for sport though – that's just too close to collecting money for myself!'

Along with other students during the Loughborough rag, Tanni threw herself into the spirit of fundraising, joining in running around collecting money from the good folk of Loughborough.

'I've been dressed up as a rabbit, dressed up as a chicken, and in one fund-raising event I remember half of us were dressed up as chickens, the other half as eggs. We've had a bike relay and on one occasion we went around in a big double-decker bus.

'Of course, being in a wheelchair, dressed as a rabbit, raised a lot of money at the student rag because people felt sorry for me. And because I was raising money for others, not myself, I was prepared to take advantage of that. I don't regret it, but I wouldn't do it now.

'Money-raising at university was fun for a variety of reasons, not least the social life and travelling round the country as a group. When, for example, we travelled around on a bus it was an absolute shambles. We had a load of mattresses on the top deck where we all dossed down in sleeping bags and would turn up outside the houses of people that we knew and borrow their bathroom.

We cadged food off people and one guy was brilliant at going to shops and saying "We're from Loughborough University. We're trying to raise money for charity, have you got any spare food you're throwing out?" He'd do this at closing time at bakeries, and supermarkets on a Saturday, and it was amazing how much food we were given.

'We lived very cheaply and ate a lot of pizza because the pizza places would invite all twenty of us in for a meal. People were so generous. They really didn't mind twenty or so students turning up, dressed as all sorts of weird animals and begging meals. They just appreciated the good fun of it all.

'In Worcester however we were thrown out of town by the

police. We were collecting money for Mencap and a local Mencap official reported us for not having a licence. We did always try to apply for licences when we could, but on some occasions we just turned up spontaneously in a place and started collecting. When the Worcester police warned us that if we didn't leave quickly they'd arrest us, we immediately packed up and moved off.

'One student raised thousands of pounds a year on his own. He did it because he believed it was something that God had asked him to do. He would jump up first thing in the morning and announce that we were going to have a prayer. The rest of us would half join in, then he would charge off to get on with the day's business. He sang Welsh hymns on the bus and was an amazing motivator.

'Everyone I knew at that time was involved in raising money. They genuinely wanted to do something good and useful and benefit the world. How I would react now if twenty or so students descended on my house I don't know. I hope I would remember how I felt as a student.'

As well as raising money for the PDSA and supporting specific disability charities, such as through her work with John Grooms, Tanni has also been involved in the annual BBC television *Children in Need* appeal.

This has had its share of controversy because a number of disabled people feel that it is demeaning for 'the disabled' to appear on television appealing for money. Conscious of this criticism, the BBC has brought in many more disabled people as consultants and has toned down what was, in the past, seen as patronizing behaviour. Tanni admits that she has mixed feelings about the programme.

Half of me says the Government is not giving enough money to people who need it, so the role of something like *Children in Need* is positive. The other half dislikes the way it pulls on heart strings.'

This dilemma remains at the centre of Tanni's life and is one she frequently wrestles with.

'I know as an athlete I could raise an awful lot more money for myself if I went out and raised money as "Tanni Grey – the poor little cripple who wants to have a go at sport" rather than as "Tanni Grey – the athlete". But I want to be sponsored as an athlete or I'm not interested. Getting the right balance to enhance the image of disabled people is very difficult.'

CHAPTER 5

A golden summer

'Fighting to control my nerves, I waited at the starting line. It had taken seven years of hard training to get there. This was it ... the big race.'

HALF PAST ELEVEN, a little earlier than anticipated, eight world-class women athletes take their marks in the Olympic stadium in Barcelona. It is the 2nd August, half-way through the Olympic Games of 1992. A huge crowd, each person considering it a privilege to be attending such a great event, falls silent. After what seems like an eternity to the athletes, the starting gun fires.

Wearing Number 2497, and her country's colours, Tanni Grey makes the first great effort she needs to begin rolling from a standing start. She knows she cannot start as quickly as some of the other stronger women, but soon she is into her stride. Her rhythm builds up. She also knows that, after two laps and almost two minutes of racing in this class of company, she cannot expect to be first across the line. It is a dream fulfilled just to be here, taking part, in the Olympic Games, before an Olympic crowd.

But this is not a dream. It is the Olympics of 1992 and Tanni Grey has been selected to take part in the women's wheel-chair exhibition event at a full Olympiad.

The result confirms the form. Barely two seconds separate the competitors but Connie Hansen is without doubt the outstanding competitor. The Danish athlete wins the event in a new world record time of 1 minute 52.62 seconds; 5.13 seconds later Tanni crosses the line. She is last and eighth but is not disappointed – all other seven competitors have a classification advantage.

127

Tanni soaks up the atmosphere knowing that, once the Olympics are over, she will be back in the stadium, not for a demonstration event but for the real thing, the Paralympic events for which she has been constantly training since her back operation over three years ago.

Barcelona in the Olympic summer of 1992 was the place to be. For those who can say, in the words Max Boyce coined to describe Wales's triumphs on the rugby pitch, '… I was there', will never forget the buzz of the city and of the occasion. It was a buzz which the Paralympians felt immediately on arriving in the city, even though the full Olympic Games were over.

The Barcelona Games may well be looked back upon as the high spot for the Paralympic movement. Sadly, negotiations to repeat the success in Atlanta in 1996 have been fraught with complications and disappointment. At Barcelona however, the Paralympians felt that they had at last found recognition as sportsmen and women.

The Olympic stadium in Barcelona had crowds queuing each day, waiting to get in to watch the events. The track saw moments of high drama unmatched even by the Olympic Games. Those who witnessed the spectacular high-speed crash in one of the men's wheelchair races will never forget the moment. Pictures of it were flashed around the world. Never before had the Paralympic Games received such prominence; never before had the world's media been so interested – and never before had the elite of the Paralympic movement been afforded the star treatment normally associated with able-bodied athletes.

The eye of the broadcasting world was on the main stadium and the Olympic pool. Even the more specialist sports, such as Boccia, in which sportsmen and women with cerebral palsy took part, attracted genuine interest and attention.

The crowd and the media were eager for stars and personalities to emerge and the golden girl was, without doubt, Tanni Grey. These things do not, of course, happen entirely haphazardly. Behind any surge in popularity there is a public relations consultant and, as *The Times* reported on 7 September, the increased public awareness of the Games in Britain had been brought about by the British Paralympic Association promoting six athletes from different sports:

> *As one of the chosen few, Grey is coming to terms with her new-found fame fitting in interviews around her racing schedule. "We have to do something to get ourselves taken seriously."*

Tanni had every quality required for the role. Not only was she a superb athlete and the top of her field, not only did she win an astonishing collection of medals, but she had the looks, personality and character to back up her achievement.

At that time, with everything poised to happen, the Paralympic movement needed Tanni as much as she needed the Paralympic Games. When a full-colour photograph of her wheeling at speed was published, in almost poster size, on the front of the *Daily Telegraph*'s sports section, it became evident that, for the first time, the Paralympic Games had acquired glamour. They were no longer, in a phrase often used by Tanni, 'cripples doing their best'. Tanni became a celebrity.

Chris Hallam who was also one of the promoted athletes does not however feel that the British Paralympic organizers were as well organized and professional as they might have been. Their chief concern had been to raise money to send the team over and he is not sure how whole-heartedly the six chosen athletes were promoted. Some also felt that promoting people like him and Tanni was not necessarily the best way to raise money.

'Perhaps they could have raised more money from using the sympathy kick.'

This was the perennial dilemma existing – should the elite be promoted as athletes, or should others be promoted for their disabilities?

Unlike four years before, selection to go to Barcelona was almost an unnecessary formality for Tanni. Already a major force in the sport and a known personality who was only too willing to do her bit on the advance publicity front, her seat on the plane to Barcelona had been guaranteed for at least three years. Just a day before leaving for Barcelona she joined fellow athlete, Ian Hayden, in collecting a £200,000 cheque from sponsors Royal Mail to go towards the British team. On the track at Barcelona however she turned from being the leading personality in a fairly closed world to being a highly recognized sports star on the national and international scene.

Tanni was joined in Barcelona by her father Peter, her sister Sian and by Andy, the boyfriend she had met at Loughborough university.

'We knew we might not see much of her, but we wanted to be there to give her our support,' says Peter. 'Our part was to give her a sense of family and the security that there was someone there to clap her or to criticize her afterwards.'

Not that Peter criticizes Tanni often. He just says if she's going to win she has got to win well and in style. On the occasions when she does not win, and feels she could have done better, she is not a good loser. Her family always knows when she is dissatisfied with herself because her voice instantly loses its sparkle. When they arrived in Barcelona, little did Peter and Sian realize that losing at these Games was not on the agenda.

Their arrival in Barcelona did not however start well. Much to their annoyance they found that they were booked into a hotel that was two-and-a-half hours away from the stadium. Far too much of their time was spent travelling to and from the action.

Sulwen stayed at home, unable as usual to bear the tension of watching her daughter race. Indeed she has never watched her daughter race at a top level. She cannot bring herself to watch any race in progress.

'I kept in touch via Radio 5 Live which used to broadcast results at 6.25 pm every evening. Sian, as the designated phoner, also kept me up to date.'

Tanni's first event at the Paralympics was a 400-metres heat, an afternoon event. As an experienced international competitor it should have presented her with no problems or worries, but she still went through her usual pre-race routine of feeling ill.

One of the team coaches with her at the time started panicking, Tanni looked so green and ill. Unaware that this was Tanni's normal practice, he went to find her family.

'She's about to throw up,' he told them anxiously.

And, when Sian responded with 'So what?', he became quite distraught.

He went running back and this time started to worry about the stadium being so full. 'Yes, sure it is,' Tanni said not believing him.

She had not heard any of the cheering when she was outside the stadium and, now inside prior to the event, she was cut off from the atmosphere in the arena. Not surprisingly, she was absolutely astonished when she came up the ramp into the stadium and found that the stadium really was full.

'I thought "Oh, my God". Then, as I went up to the start, I looked around and saw my sister and my dad in the crowds waving a huge Union Jack and a huge Welsh flag. I couldn't really miss them. It was brilliant because every time I went into the stadium after that, however packed it was, I could easily pick out the people I wanted to see. Every time I raced I knew exactly where my family and Andy were.'

Tanni knew she was hitting top form when, in her first heat, she broke the world record for the 400 metres. The huge screen of lights at the end of the stadium flashed up the news and a huge roar went up.

She completed a lap of honour to rapturous applause, and was then brought down to earth by a Spanish official tapping his watch to indicate that she should leave the track so that the next heat could be run.

In the 400 metres heat, TW3 classification, Tanni Grey's new world record of 59.20 seconds was the first time that the one-minute barrier had been broken. Ingrid Lauridsen, of Denmark, was second, nearly two seconds behind. Tanni had broken the world record, set earlier that year at 1 minute 3 seconds. The photograph of Tanni finishing does not show a single other wheelchair in sight as she crosses the line.

Sulwen heard the news by chance on Radio Wales: '… and news from the Paralympics, the first world record has been broken … by Tanni Grey!'

Sulwen leapt up with a shriek.

Peter admits to tears of elation, emotion and shock. 'It's difficult to put my feelings into words. Tanni moved from the start quite quickly, had the lead by 200 metres, and then just pulled away. In one minute, as I watched, I went from anticipation to elation. And then they announced the record. I couldn't believe that it was happening to someone in our family.'

The next day, 5 September, just over twenty-four hours after breaking her own world record, Tanni was on the track again for the 400-metres final. As number 381, she drew Lane 4 between Canadian Colette Bourgonje and Ireland's Heather O'Hare. Her main rival, Ingrid Lauridsen, was in Lane 6. When the gun went off, winning a Gold was more important than breaking a world record, and when Tanni crossed the line 0.38 seconds slower than her semi-final time she had still beaten Ingrid by 2.5 seconds.

'Fighting to control my nerves, I waited at the starting line. It had taken me seven years of hard training to get there. This was it … the big race.

'Was it all worth it? I began to wonder. I could feel 50,000 pairs of eyes on me and pushed the thought from my mind. I had to concentrate on the race.

'The starting pistol fired; we were off! I had a good start and picked up speed well. My main opponent Ingrid Lauridsen of Denmark was at my side.

'But I kept my nerve and pulled ahead of everyone else. I had to win. I couldn't let all those long hours of training on the roads around my home in Cardiff go to waste. At the final straight I was well in front and moved easily over the finishing line. I knew that I'd won, but I hardly dared to believe it so the first thing I did was look up at the electronic score-board.'

The official result was Tanni Grey, 59.58 seconds, just outside her new world record; Lauridsen from Denmark was second with

1 minute 1.91 seconds; the Italian Porcellato was third with 1 minute 3.65 seconds.

'The next thing I knew, I was off on a lap of honour around the stadium. I waved proudly at the cheering crowds, some of whom were holding out huge Union Jacks. I looked up at the spot where I knew my family would be and, seeing them, gave them a big wave. I had not only won my first Gold medal, I was now also the first woman to have won the 400 metres in a wheelchair in under a minute – the previous record before the Games had been my 63 seconds.'

In a way that seldom happened before at Paralympic Games, Tanni was swamped by the media shortly after she had crossed the line. Television and radio reporters jostled for interviews, photographers scrambled to capture the moment. Then, hustled off the track again, to make way for the next event, Tanni had to make do with only a closed-circuit television view of the Games before the medal ceremony.

Did the television close-up, which flashed on to the screen for the crowd to see, reveal a tear of pride in Tanni's eye as the National Anthem was played? Her father often remembers the moment.

'I felt as emotional as anything, suddenly thinking there's one of the Grey family who's won a Gold medal for Great Britain. You can only hope and wish for such a moment, then suddenly it's hap-pened and it's like winning the football pools.'

That night however Tanni could not afford to overdo the celebrations. The very next day she would be on the track again, this time in the final of the 100 metres. She was also only too aware that, in competing against T4 athletes, she would be at a disadvantage in the sprints. This was due to the limitations imposed on her starting speed by the lack of strength in her spine.

Yet this time, in Lane 5 with Colette Bourgonje and Evy Gundersen on either side, Tanni knew the conditions were right for a good race. There was a light wind coming towards her, but the weather was otherwise fine.

She crossed the line 17.55 seconds after the starter's gun, having once again broken one of her own world records. Ingrid Lauridsen and Colette Bourgonje were close behind. In the opening stages, with only inches separating her from Ingrid Lauridsen, Tanni's power showed at the half-way point when she stormed to the line.

Medal number two was under her belt. The scoreboard once again switched, during the detailed results, to flashing the two simple words 'world record'. Again Tanni was engulfed by the media. It was a British double in the 100 metres T3 class, with Andrew Hodge pushing past the Australian John Lindsey to clinch the gold.

The *Daily Telegraph*'s correspondent noted that both athletes had produced their personal bests.

> *Grey, who had a poor start and at 50 metres was one-and-a-half lengths behind Ingrid Lauridsen (Denmark) kept her nerve and rhythm and gradually closed the distance. With 20 metres to go she drew level and edged ahead to win.*

The *Daily Telegraph* also pointed out that Tanni Grey had trained regularly with the men's team and this she believed was an important factor in being able to produce explosive bursts when they were really need.

> *This showed in the 400 metres on Saturday. She was well clear of the field half-way down the back straight and allowed herself to cruise home … but it was sheer mental grit that brought her the 100-metres gold.*

Afterwards Tanni admitted that the race had been almost too close for comfort.

When she and the other five athletes lined up for the semi-final of the 200 metres on 9 September, there seemed little doubt to onlookers that, on form and on paper, Tanni would have no problems at all. Her qualifying time and new world record of

31.04 seconds was four seconds faster than any of her rivals, even Ingrid Lauridsen. Racing in Lane 6, Tanni set a new Paralympic record of 32.78 seconds.

Such was the tightness of the schedule that, only five hours later, Tanni was back on the track for the final. With Tracey Lewis failing to qualify in her semi-final, Tanni was the only British representative among the eight.

At 5.52 am, the results board flashed the news that Tanni had been waiting for. Another Gold. And she had broken the Paralympic record yet again, beating Ingrid Lauridsen by almost a second.

The next day, in clear contrast to four years before, the British newspapers carried the news in a major way. No longer was the Paralympic Games receiving a few column inches: *Tanni wins third gold with record* was the headline which greeted readers of the next morning's papers.

Sulwen was getting calls from the Press, requesting quotes to express her delight and joy. Friends and neighbours were also calling with their congratulations; Uncle Ivor was just one who had watched Tanni race from junior level and who loved to see her out and about training. He could barely contain his pleasure over the news: 'It was such an exciting time' he confessed.

There was more to come – the final of the women's 800 metres in the TW3 class. Could Tanni repeat her Olympic form where, despite coming third, she had set a new world record for her class with her time of 1 minute 57.75 seconds?

'It was a very close race,' Peter said, 'but Tanni was taken at the line by the American girl. For quite a while I thought that Tanni had failed to get her fourth Gold. Then the scoreboard flashed the result. Tanni had won. It was a shock to the entire stadium. Ann Cody had been disqualified.'

Once again with Ingrid Lauridsen, the Silver girl of the Games, coming second, Tanni had won the final, setting a new Paralympic record of 2 minutes 6.58 seconds. But controversy tarnished the final Gold because Tanni had not crossed the line first.

An 800 metres race has a staggered start with all athletes racing in lanes to begin with until the field breaks and each competitor has to jockey for the best position. At 120 metres Tanni realized that, although she had done well and was ahead of the field, she was tiring and the world record was no longer a possibility. She kept the lead until halfway through, but at the bell began to falter. Ann Cody of the United States overtook her on the final bend and she could not respond.

Tanni came second and, for five minutes, experienced the disappointment of failure. Sian, watching from the grandstand, shared her disappointment.

'I was upset, thinking it was a Silver. We watched as Ann Cody did a lap of honour and Tanni came off the track.'

Turning to go back to the changing rooms and marshalling area, Tanni paused for a brief word with a television interviewer and then continued on, in order to pack up her kit. Then she noticed two American coaches talking to Ann Cody, and heard Ann shouting, 'What's happened? What's happened? What do you mean?'

'Then somebody came over to me and said "Have you heard?" And I said "Heard what?" And they told me that Ann had been disqualified because she had broken a couple of metres too early.'

Tanni in fact was one of the last to know that, following a judge's objection, officials had announced that Ann Cody and Tracey Lewis had been disqualified for breaking too early, and that the Gold medal was awarded to her.

Tanni was also credited with the new Paralympic record time, but by that time she was too exhausted after seven days of fierce competition and pressure to really appreciate the news.

That she should receive a fourth Gold in such circumstances was not ideal. The rules however had to be observed and in the judges' opinion both Tracey and Ann had moved from their lanes and begun to challenge for the best position too early. There was also disappointment that, after discussions, Tanni had to give up her attempt at a world record.

'I saw Ann after the race and she was incredibly upset,' Tracey Lewis says describing the events of the day. 'If it had been me I would have felt awfully cheated. But rules are rules and, although there was no deliberate flouting of them, the rules had to be enforced. I must admit that, given the circumstances, if I had been Tanni I would not have been able to accept the Gold for myself.

'Ann found it very hard,' Tanni says, 'but she stayed for the medal ceremony. It was very difficult for me, too. I wanted to go up, talk to her and say "I'm sorry. It's not the way I would have chosen to win a Gold, and it must be really horrible for you to have the medal taken away".

'I remember coming out from the medal ceremony and looking up at the stands where Ann was watching with one of her friends. It must have been really hard for her to come to that ceremony and I had a lot of respect for her. My feelings were very mixed. I knew how bad she must be feeling and yet I was relieved that I had won four Gold medals. She didn't cheat. She just lost concentration at the wrong point. Tracey saw Ann break and followed.

'I felt I hadn't had a good race,' says Tanni, 'and that I'd been a bit naive in the way I'd run it. I'd already done a lot of racing and was quite tired. I was disappointed in myself when Ann crossed the line in front of me.

'Looking back on it all now, I still feel sorry for her but she should have known where the line was and there's no excuse for breaking before the line.'

The Games had other controversial moments. A British javelin thrower fell under suspicion for drug-taking, but was able to demonstrate that he was taking drugs only for medicinal purposes. However, a Hungarian shot-putter was stripped of a Silver medal and banned from further competition for drug abuse. The shot-putter was found to have traces of the anabolic steroid Methandienone in his sample.

The Games' chief medical officer, Michael Riding, saw the advent of cheating as inevitable. 'As the stakes get higher,' he explained, 'the temptations will grow. Able-bodied athletes have just been at it longer and have more resources.

'There are always a few people trying to get into a more favourable disability class. We have sent several athletes home for not reaching the standards for minimal disability'.

To round off the amazing Games, Tanni helped the British relay team to a Silver medal. Rose Hill, also one of the Squad, believes that the British could have won and that only failing to work together sufficiently as a team prevented them from doing so. In the event however, the winning margin recorded by the Americans was so great that it would have taken considerable dedication and concentration for the British Squad to have done that.

The relay is not Tanni's favourite event and, while she had agreed to take part, winning it was not one of her key goals for Barcelona. The British Squad had only come together a short while before the race and, for some time, there was doubt as to whether the relay would take place at all. Tanni believes it should have been cancelled because there were not enough entries to make it viable. The Irish were only brought in at the last minute, fielding little more than a scratch team.

'We were completely outclassed by the Americans who finished 50 metres ahead of us. We were a similar distance ahead of the Mexicans who were third and the Irish were disqualified, being inexperienced in changeovers. It is not the way that a Paralympic event should be organized.'

In the personal medal table, Tanni came third behind the American Bart Dodson, whose tally of six Gold medals outstripped everybody elses, and Rimma Batalova who, with four Gold medals and one Silver, only crept ahead of Tanni when the names were arranged in alphabetical order. A triumph for Tanni but for others something of a disappointment.

Ian Thompson was one athlete who had a very disappointing time, crashing in the 1500 metres, injuring an elbow and missing the relay. His memories of the impressive Games however and of its huge, enthusiastic crowds still remain extremely positive.

By the end of the Games, Tanni's official curriculum vitae, printed out by the Paralympic computer, was one of the most impressive. She was the holder of six major records: the world records in the 100, 200, 400 and 800 metres, and the Paralympic record holder in all four of her events. The biography also entered under its personal details that Tanni's weight was recorded at 45 kilos and her height at 163 centimetres. It recorded her profession as being in full-time sports training and mentioned that at her Cardiff club Tanni averaged six hours of training every day. Within her category, it also recorded that she was, without doubt, the fastest woman wheelchair athlete in the world.

In the *Sunday Times* immediately after the Games, Rupert Widdicombe wrote:

> *Four years ago in Seoul children had to be given a day off school, bussed to the stadium and told what country to cheer for to supply a little atmosphere. But in Barcelona it was different.*
>
> *The stadium was on several occasions packed with up to 55,000 people who had not come to be "nice to the disabled", as one competitor put it, but to see athletics of the highest calibre.*
>
> *On weekday afternoons there have been two-hour queues for the swimming events – even after the organizers had re-opened a temporary stand built specially for the Olympics. Watching in all venues over the last eleven days have been people who at first may have muttered "what's wrong with her?" to gradually become affected by an atmosphere that was truly exciting.*

It was true that the Games seemed to have taken on a new status. The new high-perfomance wheelchairs were now moving faster than Olympic runners in events of 800 metres and above. The *Sunday Times* article explained the appeal of the Games as being because:

> *…they are genuinely exciting, at times spectacular and occasionally dangerous.*

Three men were taken to hospital after an eight-chair pile-up in one 5000 metre event. It has also dawned on an increasingly knowledgeable audience that they are witnessing some supreme athletic performances by any standard.

Forty years on from its humble beginnings, it looks like the Paralympic Games have come of age. One-legged high-jumpers can clear 2 metres. One-armed runners cover the 1500 metres in times that would have earned them places in the semi-finals of the Olympics, and world Paralympic records have been broken in two-thirds of the events.

Ajibola Adeoye's one-armed 10.7 second 100 metre was faster than some of the sprinters in the Nigerian Olympic team, whose attempts to recruit him were roundly rebuffed.

As that year's London Marathon winner and a star of the Paralympics, Tanni's comments were sought for the article. She told the paper how things had changed since Seoul. Then, it had been common for athletes to compete in every distance, from sprints to the marathons whereas, increasingly, athletes now had to specialize in the larger events in order to stand a chance. 'People are now training much harder,' she summarised, emphasising the substantial financial rewards that were also now available, expecially in the US.

The Barcelona Paralympics represented an enormous success. The International Olympic Committee president, Juan Antonio Samaranch, promised to push for the inclusion of seventy-nine full medal events for the Paralympic athletes in the Atlanta Olympics. There had been just two demonstration events in all of the last three Games.

The *Sunday Times* article concluded however that the Paralympic Games should be wary of its own achievement:

It seems the hurdle of being taken seriously has been leaped. But the mire of classification, drugs and the separations of these Games from the Olympics are issues that will run and run.

It was indeed a very fair summing up of the Games. They had been a tremendous success yet this triumph brought with it a whole new set of problems. The very emergence of elite athletes, like Tanni, meant that there were problems ahead which would need to be tackled before the next Games in Atlanta.

CHAPTER SIX

Awards and honours

*'I am not into demonstrations and waving banners. I
want to tackle attitudes by showing people I am not
incapacitated or stupid.'*

MANY ATHLETES DREAM of, but few can anticipate winning a
Gold medal at the very highest level. Understandably when this
happens, there is joy and elation, tears and laughter, and
rewards, ranging from the financial to those that money cannot
buy.

The congratulations and celebrations had started as soon as
Tanni returned home to Wales after the Barcelona Games.
Having been held up at Heathrow airport, when she discovered
that her racing chair had been sent on a separate flight, she did
not actually arrive home until nightfall.

The next day she found bunting and balloons decorating the
front of her home in Cardiff and a huge Union Jack in the
window. There were also piles of messages awaiting her.
Everybody it seemed who had in any way been associated with her
success, wished to offer their congratulations. These were heady
days. Indeed, from the moment she arrived back in Wales, and
for the rest of the year, it was one long round of awards, honours
and celebrations.

'May I congratulate you on behalf of the Sports Council for
Wales on your splendid achievements,' wrote Ossie Wheatley,
Chairman of the Council.

'I am writing on behalf of the British Paralympic Association
to congratulate you for the excellent overall performance of the

Great Britain team in Barcelona,' wrote the President of the Association, Dr Adrian Whiteson.

And from the BPA Athletics Committee, Martin Mansell wrote, 'I would like to congratulate you on your success in the Barcelona Paralympics ... well done.'

On 15 October the South Glamorgan Health Authority passed a special resolution instructing the Chairman to write to Peter Grey to convey their congratulations to his daughter. And, less formally, from the Sports Council for Wales, Nick Whitehead wrote to them simply in his own hand, 'Welcome home! Well done!'

Among the letters from family and friends were also invitations and other surprises. On 14 October, Tanni heard that she was the winner of the *Sunday Times* Disabled Sportswoman Award. She had assumed that the women's open category was a foregone conclusion, with Sally Gunnell the Olympic athlete taking the award.

When Tanni's name was announced as the *Sunday Times* Sportswoman of the Year as well, she was 'genuinely amazed'. The prize was £1000. She also received an invitation to BBC television's *Sports Review of the Year* programme and to the 'People of the Year' luncheon at RADAR.

Little could Tanni have anticipated that six months after winning four Gold medals in Barcelona, she would be a guest of honour at London Zoo naming a newly born giraffe after herself! It is a tradition at London Zoo to name giraffes born at Regent's Park after sporting personalities. The names of the half-sisters and half-brothers of Tanni's giraffe include 'Linford', 'Henry' after Henry Cooper, 'Gary' after Lineker, and 'Annabel' after Annabel Croft.

Young 'Tanni' was born on 28 November to a mother called 'Crackers' (obviously not born at the Zoo) and a father called 'Hilary' named after Sir Edmund. In the same giraffe enclosure were newly-born 'Graham' after the cricketer Graham Gooch, and 'Sally' named after Sally Gunnell. Tanni was invited to the Zoo to meet her taller namesake and to give the press a photo opportunity. Sian's sisterly observation on this occasion was that it would have been more appropriate if the animal had been a monkey!

The giraffe's reaction to the razzmatazz of the naming ceremony is not recorded. Tanni however accepted this celebration of her success with her customary gratitude, professionalism and a cheery good humour.

One London celebration that Tanni missed was organized by the Royal Mail to honour the Olympic and Paralympic stars. This resulted in an embarrassing, but to many of the Paralympians hugely amusing, gaffe by the sports commentator David Coleman. Held the day after her return, Tanni, having only received an informal invitation, decided to give the occasion a miss because it would involve a long journey from Wales to London and she was in need of a rest.

The story goes that David Coleman, hosting the event, called for Tanni to come forward to receive an award. When there was no response, he called her name again. The third time he tried a different tack. 'If Miss Tanni Grey is present, would she please stand up'!

A few days later Peter and Sulwen held an open house party and people, responding to the buzz of excitement, dropped in even if they barely knew the Greys. 'Everybody got to know everybody and it was all very exciting.'

Amid the celebration and the congratulations however there was worry concerning Tanni's relationship with Andy. He had travelled to Barcelona and kept in touch with Tanni as much as he could during the Games but as she was pursuing each event with single-minded determination, she was unable to spend as much time with him as he would have liked. The little spare time she did have available was spent with Sian and her father.

As with so many relationships, after a period when all appears to be going well, tensions had surfaced. Tanni knew that after Barcelona she could go on to achieve many more things and there was no question in her mind of giving up and resting on her laurels. Sulwen and Peter had become very fond of Andy but they felt that he tended to be over-protective and that this was not something Tanni wanted or required.

'For the whole of 1992 there were problems between us,' Tanni recalls 'and Andy wasn't really happy with me being away.

'He was always very protective, which was okay when we were at Loughborough but university is not the real world. It was easy to spend lots of time together while we were enclosed in this little bubble but by 1992 we were spending more and more time apart. I was doing things in Cardiff and he was still in his final year at Loughborough.

'It just wasn't working out for either of us. We were spending more and more time arguing about nothing. By then, we had also become very different people. I believe he thought I was going to quit racing after Barcelona, but I had no plans to do that.

'It was particularly difficult during the Games because Andy wanted us to spend time together and I couldn't. When I am competing I am not very sociable. I need to lock myself away. Perhaps Andy also didn't like the fact that the rest of the team were always around. He wanted to see me on his own and that was not possible.'

'In the last couple of days in Barcelona I knew there was no point in kidding myself any longer that our relationship was going to work. There had been problems for some time and I made the decision to get out rather than for us to continue hurting each other.'

By the end of the Barcelona Games, Tanni had also acquired celebrity status and became public property. She had previously experienced what this involved, albeit in a more modest way, after the Seoul Games and after her 1992 London Marathon win. But she now says that she went through the weeks after Barcelona in a 'bit of a dream'.

'Another invitation would arrive and I'd think "Yes, I'd like to go to that. That sounds really nice". Looking back now on late 1992 and early 1993, I still say "Wow! Is that ever going to happen again?" So many good things happened. I won the Welsh Sports

Personality Award, the *Sunday Times* Sportswoman of the Year and was invited on to *Question of Sport*. I remember the producer ringing up and asking me if I could possibly spare the time to be on the programme. I must have sounded very cool, pretending to look at my diary to see if it was alright. When I put the phone down, having accepted the invitation, I looked at mum and said "Guess what?"'

Appearing on this programme, with Bill Beaumont and Frank Bruno against Ian Botham's team, brought her immediate public recognition from people who had not followed the Paralympic Games.

'After the programme, all the men who spoke to me wanted to know what Ian Botham was like and all the women wanted to know about Roger Black, who was in Ian's team. It was good fun and a great opportunity.'

Tanni also found herself pictured on the celebrity page of *Hello* magazine in October 1992, given equal billing with Lord and Lady Romsey, Mr and Mrs George Bush, Kirk Douglas and Dustin Hoffman! Even if she had wanted to retire from the celebrity spotlight and settle down quietly with Andy, it would have been difficult to arrange.

There was no let-up either from racing and training and on the 3rd of October, Tanni was at Porthcawl for the British Wheelchair Road Championships. Eight laps of a 3.259 mile circuit, plus the finishing straight, made up the 26 miles 385 yards of the traditional marathon course. From the point of view of encouraging crowds to attend the event, Tanni was the chief attraction and a number of her fellow Paralympic athletes competed with her, including Chris Hallam, Rose Hill and Tracey Lewis.

By November the invitations following her success at the Paralympic Games were turning into events. The People of the Year luncheon, for example, held at the London Hilton on Park Lane on 11 November, started at eleven o'clock and went on well into the afternoon.

Speakers included Lady Margaret Thatcher, Ned Sherin and

Brian Redhead. The South Wales press was quick to spot that three of fourteen awards that year had gone to people from South Wales. As well as Tanni, there was the passenger in a light aircraft who had taken over the controls and landed safely when the pilot had a heart attack and a police officer who had rescued a Jack Russell terrier from the jaws of a Pit Bull in a playground of young children.

Tanni, with what was described by the *South Wales Echo* as 'typical modesty', said in her speech: 'I enjoy what I do, but landing a plane and tackling a ferocious dog is something else'. She then added: 'This is a big step forward for Paralympic athletes, putting them on the same footing as the able bodied. This is the first time women have been included in the awards.'

Others being honoured included speaker Betty Boothroyd, Lynda Chalker and the tennis broadcaster Dan Maskell.

It was at this lunch that the entertainer Roy Castle, who was also one of the People of the Year, hit the headlines when he refused to shake hands with Lady Thatcher because of her association with an American cigarette company. Roy Castle, who has since died from lung cancer, believed he developed the disease as a passive smoker. Tanni's souvenir programme of the lunch was signed by many of those present, including Lady Thatcher, Roy Castle, Lynda Chalker and Sally Gunnell.

A few weeks later, Tanni was at the Drapers Hall in the City of London to receive the *Sunday Times* Sportswoman of the Year Award. The whole family came with her. Having previously been a student winner, Tanni was familiar with the occasion, but to win the award with Sally Gunnell as runner-up took her completely by surprise.

Just a few days later, she was back in Wales to receive the Disabled Sports Personality of the Year award at the Welsh Paraplegic and Tetraplegic Sports Association dinner in Cardiff.

All this in a month when Tanni's athletic skills were much in demand for a *Radio Times* relay to raise money for the BBC *Children in Need* appeal. The *Children in Need* torch was taken on a 750-mile relay around the country by Tanni and a team of 'athletic stars', including Steve Cram and Linford Christie. The route went from Manchester through Cumbria, Yorkshire down to Leicestershire, Nottingham, Suffolk, Coventry and Birmingham, and there were additional legs in Scotland and Northern Ireland.

It was also in the middle of November, the 16th to be exact, that a letter was despatched from 10 Downing Street addressed to 'Miss T C D Grey'. The envelope was marked 'Urgent – Personal from the Prime Minister on Her Majesty's Service'. As Tanni was away at the time, Sulwen, who was dealing with business matters, opened the letter. Headed 'In Confidence', it was signed by the Prime Minister's Principal Private Secretary, Alex Allan.

> *The Prime Minister has asked me to inform you, in strict confidence, that he has in mind, on the occasion of the forthcoming list of New Year Honours, to submit your name to the Queen with a recommendation that Her Majesty may be graciously pleased to approve that you be appointed a Member of the Order of the British Empire.*
>
> *Before doing so, the Prime Minister would be glad to be assured that this would be agreeable to you. I should be grateful if you would let me know by completing the enclosed form and sending it to me by return of post.*
>
> *If you agree that your name should go forward and the Queen accepts the Prime Minister's recommendation, the announcement will be made in the New Year's Honours list. You will receive no further communication before the list is published.*
>
> *I am, Madam, your obedient servant, Alex Allan.*

The letter arrived the morning after Tanni had completed a four-lap leg of the BBC *Children in Need* Olympic Torch Fun Run at Cardiff Athletic Stadium, along with Steve Cram and hundreds of others who paid £1 to take part. Tanni had already set off to the next location when Sulwen caught up with her on a mobile phone. Worried that the confidential matter might be overheard, Sulwen felt she could not give Tanni the news directly and tried to think of ways of suggesting the content without letting on.

'You know Lynn Davies has got letters after his name,' she said mysteriously, referring to the celebrated Welsh Olympic long-jumper.

Tanni did not get the hint immediately, so her mother persisted with other heavy hints. In due course Tanni twigged. Not only was she to receive an MBE, but the matter had to be kept under wraps until the official New Year announcement.

'The MBE meant a lot to my parents,' she later commented. 'It means a lot to me too, as do the other awards and honours I received.'

That year, the *Children in Need* appeal was picketed by protesters at Television Centre, rekindling some of Tanni's doubts about the morality of this kind of fund-raising. Was she right to try and change attitudes from within or should she have been one of the protesters?

Writing to her at the end of November, the Events Director, John Caine, thanked her for taking part over the two-and-a-half weeks of the relay and added,

> *I would also like to thank you for teaching me more about the problems of some disabled people in a couple of weeks than I have managed to learn during the rest of my life. You were also dead right about working from within. Those protesters at Television Centre achieved nothing compared to the impact of yourself around the country.*

Sarah Tremellen, from the *Children in Need* team, also wrote to thank Tanni:

> *You and Steve worked harder than anyone, rushing around doing interviews and posing for photographs, and I never heard you complain once (perhaps you just did it when I wasn't there!) You were brilliant, thank you ever so much.*

What were the highlights of the relay for Tanni? The surprise Panasonic award handed over by Steve Cram with the cameras rolling at Sheffield? Meeting and getting to know many of the top sporting personalities from other disciplines? Or was it the time in a McDonalds in Newcastle when Tanni and the team, all in their international tracksuits, went to get a bite to eat?

'I was in my chair and my left shoe lace was undone. Steve Cram said to me, "Hey Tanni, you'll trip over in a minute." Jokingly, I told him to get lost, but then a minute later my lace got caught in the wheel and I found myself tipped out of my chair on the floor!'

Then, still in November, two other invitations turned up. The first to arrive was for Welsh Sports Personality of the Year 1992. The second, on the final day of the month, asked Tanni to be a guest in Cardiff to help launch the *Going for Gold* programme to raise money to assist talented youngsters train in their chosen sports. The money, which came via Welsh Sports Aid that year, covered twenty-two different events ranging from trampolining to squash and skiing, to motorcycling and karate.

Four days later, on 3 December, Tanni was involved in a presentation organized through Health Care Gwent on 'Gardening and Disability'. She also recorded an interview with BBC television for the *Review of the Year* programme at the same time.

Yet more letters of congratulations came in, including one from the Vice Chancellor of Loughborough University:

> *Staff and students alike have been inspired by your determination in achieving four gold medals in Barcelona this year.*

A few days later the university was writing again, this time with their invitation to become an honorary graduate. Tanni was also offered honorary life membership of the Cardiff Amateur Athletics Club, the club where she trains.

Tanni also managed during this busy time to spend three months helping produce resource and publicity material for a

BP-funded project designed to encourage disabled students to take up higher education and college opportunities.

The hectic period of public appearances was not just restricted to events connected with athletics and herself. Not long after the Paralympic Games in September Tanni, in her capacity as an appeal's volunteer for the People's Dispensary for Sick Animals, was one of the PDSA team who welcomed Princess Alexandra to the charity's shop in Cardiff. Tanni had raised £30,000 for the PDSA when she won the London Wheelchair Marathon that year.

Wanting to be involved in a voluntary organization about which she would have no qualms of conscience, she had offered her services to the PDSA. She is not a vegetarian but she detests cruelty to animals.

Then, after Christmas, the New Year's Honours list was published and, with other well-known personalities and sportsmen, Tanni was honoured alongside Roy Castle OBE, Leslie Crowther CBE, Sally Gunnell, Chris Boardman the cyclist, and England's cricket team manager, Mickey Stewart.

The award of the MBE brought in another flurry of letters of congratulation. Family, friends, the Welsh Sports Hall of Fame, RADAR, Cardiff Amateur Athletic Club, Cardiff's Lord Mayor, the Sports Council, the British Wheelchair Sports Foundation, South Glamorgan County Council, the Commonwealth Games Council for Wales and many others all wrote.

On the award of her MBE, the *South Wales Echo* wrote a leader. It saluted the other Welsh recipients of honours and added:

Pride of place must go to the disabled athlete Tanni Grey, who won four gold medals at the Paralympics and so deservedly gets the MBE. Tanni is an inspiration to everyone in a wheelchair – proof that with courage and endeavour almost anything can be achieved.

"I'm delighted because young disabled people don't have many role models," she said modestly.

They do today, Tanni, as we move into 1993 you are an inspiration to us all.

In January, Tanni took Sian to the Sports Aid Foundation Dinner at the great hall of London's Guildhall where tribute was to be paid to those who had achieved top success in Barcelona.

The Sports Aid Foundation, through its charitable arm, the Sports Foundation Charitable Trust, helps many thousands of youngsters to enjoy sport and achieve their best.

Among those attending the dinner was Tanni's fellow para-lympian, Beverley Gull, athlete Derek Redmond and swimmers Sharon Davies, Duncan Goodhew and Adrian Moorhouse.

Later, in the same month, Tanni was honoured again by the local press when the *Western Mail* in conjunction with BBC Wales, elected her the Welsh Sports Personality of the Year. She was the first disabled athlete to win the coveted trophy, but was unable to be at the ceremony at St Davids Hall in Cardiff because she was in Australia taking part in a race. For this reason, the huge silver trophy was presented to her earlier by the actor Sir Anthony Hopkins.

'I've won several awards in recent months,' Tanni said at the time, 'but this one means more to me than any of the others because I've won it as an athlete and not as a disabled person.'

She had held off a strong challenge from Ian Rush, the footballer, and the boxer Bobby Reagan to become the thirty-ninth winner of the award.

The race in Australia was the Oz Day 10 km Wheelchair Race sponsored by the Sheraton Wentworth Hotel, which is where Tanni stayed. It attracted substantial, at least in Paralympic terms, prize money. The winning man was to receive A$3,000 and the winning woman A$2,000. In addition, the T2 and T1 classes and the juniors were to receive their own awards. There were thirty-five women taking part joining the seventy-four men on the track. Connie Hansen and Ingrid Lauridsen from Denmark, Louise Sauvage from Australia, together with Tanni were the main attractions.

There was a considerable build up for the event and the day before, hundreds of spectators turned out to watch the athletes training in Sydney's Centennial park. The event was broadcast by

ABC and media facilities were made available for interviews after the race, much as happens for a Grand Prix event on the able-bodied athletes' calendar. Attended by the New South Wales Governor, it was clearly a major event for the city. Louise Sauvage, to the delight of a partisan crowd, won with Tanni coming in fourth.

Then, back from the sunshine, Tanni launched into more engagements nearer home. Typical of these was a February visit to Mold in Wales where Tanni, as guest of honour at the Alun School, officially opened the swimming pool hoist designed to enable disabled people to use the swimming facilities at the town sports centre. In a round of schools, she also went to Denby and spoke to the PE students and visiting pupils from Ysgol Golgarth in Llandudno.

Tanni enjoys these opportunities to discuss disability with children.

'They are far more open than adults,' she says. 'and have no qualms about asking a whole range of questions that adults might feel are too personal. I get a lot of really intelligent questions and some fairly awkward ones. If they ask me how I go to the toilet, I tell them. They also want to know how much I get paid to race and always want to try out the racing chair. They also want to know if I've met Linford Christie or Kriss Akabusi.'

At the end of February, Tanni was back at the airport checking in for another transatlantic flight. This time she was on her way to the 15-km wheelchair race at the city of Tampa in Florida. Like the London Marathon, this is an event in which both wheelchair athletes and runners compete on the same course.

Two days later, on St David's Day, she won a 10-km race in the Florida heat – her third race in three days. Then, while telephoning home to tell her parents of her success, she was given the news that she had gained a Winston Churchill travelling fellowship.

Tanni had applied to the Winston Churchill Memorial Trust earlier, and the award meant a great deal to her. She had been selected to receive one of the 1993 Winston Churchill travelling fellowships to enable her to visit Australia for eight weeks to study sport. Like all top British athletes, the wheelchair elite take every opportunity to spend the winter abroad where training facilities are often superior and they can miss the vagaries of a British winter.

Originally Tanni had thought of going to Illinois but she opted to work with Jenny Banks and Louise Sauvage in Perth, Western Australia instead. The award, worth £5000, was in the 'sport and young leaders under 25' category. There was stiff competition from lots of other Olympic athletes, hoping for the money to enable them to study and train in the sunshine.

Tanni often reflects that she is privileged in never having had to take a proper job. The only conventional job she has held was as a student, when she worked briefly for the Cardiff-based MEM group of companies. This mostly involved office computer work and the boss, Mike McGraine has kept in touch with her career ever since.

Tanni's role as a sports personality means that, in addition to receiving and presenting awards, she is sometimes required to be the guest speaker at various formal gatherings. Back in Wales on 13 March, she was a guest speaker, along with Glenys Kinnock, at the International Women's Day at Porth, organized by the Mid Glamorgan Community Education Women's Forum.

But, between these times, there was always the track and road circuit to get back to. On 14 March Tanni was in Portsmouth defending her title in the Portsmouth Half-Marathon. She came sixth, but was the first woman over the line in 52 minutes 27 seconds. Six athletes were separated by just four seconds at the end, although the winner Ivan Newman won comfortably. At the head of the six-strong wheelchair pack, and coming third in the event, was Ian Thompson.

The MBE investiture was the next thing to worry over. Tanni was sent strict instructions from the Central Chancery of the Orders of Knighthood at St James's Palace. Under no circumstances was photography allowed inside Buckingham Palace. Under no circumstances was Tanni to arrive later than 10.50 am.

She was permitted to bring two guests with her and she was to wear day dress. She chose a navy hat and green tartan dress. Peter and Sulwen were determined not to risk being late for the occasion and stayed at a hotel near Victoria the night before.

Buckingham Palace is not especially accessible to wheelchairs and Tanni had to report to a special entrance. Once there, she recalls being attended to by five or six uniformed members of the household who transferred her into a Buckingham Palace wheelchair and lifted her up the steps.

'It was all done so very properly. They even put a blanket over my knees to preserve my modesty! If it had been done by anyone else, I don't think I would have put up with it.

'I remember feeling very nervous and waiting for what appeared a long time. I realised it was a great honour and was specially pleased for my parents.'

Details culled from that day, 16 March, show the major impact the day had on them all. They remember walking along the corridors to the area where the investiture was to take place. On the way, they were met by the Director of the Churchill Fellowship who knew Tanni. She however did not immediately recognize him in his medals and smart clothes because the last time she had seen him, he had been in a pair of grey slacks and a sweater!

'We had to wait for ages,' says Sulwen. 'We were all given instructions that we mustn't clap and were told how the Queen would arrive and would be preceded by the Yeoman, what music would be played, and when we had to stand up for the National Anthem.

'We recognized some of the people who were there at the same investiture. There was John Thaw who plays Detective Morse on television and Jimmy Young. The timing was impeccable because the palace people had done it many times before.'

Sulwen recalls the knights and the CBEs and the OBEs coming before the Members of the Order of the British Empire, and certainly recollects the moment when Tanni's name was read out.

'It was a very emotional moment for us,' Sulwen recalls, 'to see Tanni enter and push herself forward. She had somebody walking behind her and, although she was nervous that her hat might fall off, it didn't. She had her moment with the Queen who asked her about her racing and about her next race. The aide, who had been on the far side and who had remained impassively sober throughout, suddenly smiled as Tanni came along, and I thought "That's nice!"'

After the award from the Queen, Tanni was invited to be a guest at St James's Palace and to make some presentations herself on behalf of Prince Philip. She was selected as one of a group of achievers to present young people with Duke of Edinburgh Gold awards. The format was that each youngster would meet the Duke of Edinburgh and, after that, a celebrity such as Tanni would present the certificates on his behalf.

Once again, detailed instructions were sent out for the royal occasion. Tanni was given permission to park her car in a coveted spot in the Mall and was told that as she arrived at St James's Palace, she would be met at the Friary Court entrance and escorted upstairs to the Tapestry room. There she would be introduced to a Gold award guide.

The instructions went on to tell her that a tour of the Palace had been arranged for everyone and that when they eventually reached the State Apartment and Prince Philip entered, everyone was to stand – a curious instruction to send to Tanni, but she appreciated what was meant! Prince Philip would then chat to the young people who would be assembled in groups of twenty-five and Tanni would be introduced as the designated presenter. Tanni was then to hand out certificates and give a short address. She was advised that as there were 100 certificates to present and she might be tempted to chat to all the young people present, a short word of congratulations would be deemed sufficient. The room steward would be on hand to advise her on how she was doing for time and to guide her through the presentation.

A detailed guide for the presenter's speech was also sent to Tanni, suggesting a maximum time of five minutes. It also explained that the award was a non-competitive award that looked at each individual's skills and abilities. They would have arrived at the awards by devoting at least two hours of their leisure time every week over two years to the scheme.

Come the spring of 1993 Tanni was entered yet again for the London Marathon, this time as defending champion. It is the one race in the year that she dreads, knowing that it will be preceded by nerves and nausea. This time she was under the media spotlight more than usual because a television crew, preparing a programme for a BBC 2 documentary on her career, was following her every move. In the event it was not a good race. The weather was bad and the conditions were far more suited to a stronger, more muscular, competitor such as Rose Hill. Rose did in fact win and Tanni finished in 3rd place.

Also in April, the Committee of the Welsh Sports Hall of Fame decided it would break with tradition and honour a sports person who was very different from any of the others honoured before. The Hall of Fame keeps its Roll of Honour at the Welsh Institute of Sport in Cardiff and, until then, only sixteen names appeared on it. These included footballers of the standing of John Charles, rugby players such as Cliff Morgan. Now, the Roll of Honour was to be expanded to include Tanni along with the snooker star Ray Reardon, boxer Eddy Thomas and the former Wales and British Lions Wing, Gerald Davies. In addition there were four posthumous names inscribed: Jimmy Wilde, Olympic gold medallist Irene Steer, George Latham and Jim Sullivan.

Two days after this event, Tanni was in London for the Sporting Awards luncheon of the Variety Club of Great Britain where, yet again, Prince Philip would be present. She was due to receive the Disabled Sportswoman of the Year award. On the same occasion, judo Gold medal winner Simon Jackson won the Disabled Sportsman Award and a special award was given to Ian Botham.

In May, as if naming a giraffe was not unusual enough, Tanni was invited to be the first person to hold and sniff a new rose, the John Grooms rose, which had been named after the national charity for disabled people. It had been specially created by a rose grower from Attleborough to mark the 127th anniversary of the John Grooms Association. The grower, Peter Beales, presented Tanni with the very first bloom which then travelled on to be seen by the connoisseurs of the Chelsea Flower Show.

The rose is of particular importance for the John Grooms charity, because when John Grooms started his mission it was directed at disabled flower-sellers in London. The early fund-raising of the organization centred around the sale of blooms as buttonholes and John Grooms produced 13 million artificial roses for the first Queen Alexandra Rose Day in 1912.

Soon after this, Tanni was once again present on the platform when the railway engine 'John Grooms' was named by Lord Tonypandy. She had had no connection with John Grooms until she was contacted by the charity, but since then she has kept up her interest.

Also in May, despite a heavy training schedule, Tanni was able to fit an important appointment into her diary – to open a new veterinary centre in Cardiff. She unveiled a plaque at the PDSA centre, in Bute Street, which included four consulting rooms, two operating theatres, recovery rooms and X-ray facilities to provide free treatment for sick and injured pets.

That year, Tanni chose as her own charity, to sponsor the Royal National Lifeboat Institute and raised £21,161. Of this, £12,000 went towards the Penarth Lifeboat Appeal. Tanni's father is the Vice Chairman of the Cardiff branch of the RNLI and so Tanni had a special personal reason for wanting to give the Institute's funds a boost.

During 1993 she was also the subject of a number of feature articles. Many of these covered old ground and familiar stories, but a few stood out as providing new insights into Tanni and her character. For example in *Young People Now*, the sub-editor, Isabel George, met what she later described in the headline as the owner of the 'fastest wheels in the west'.

The article then painted a revealing picture of Tanni the athlete.

The whiz of three slim wheels on tarmac often breaks the morning silence in the cosy Cardiff suburb where Tanni Grey lives …

Every morning she scrunches her dark bobbed hair under her helmet, wraps her lean body against the cold and takes to the road on another 10 km training session.

Dodging the city traffic is a dangerous occupation, but Tanni has been battling against the odds all her life. Born with spina bifida, and now paralysed from the waist down, Tanni was introduced to her wheelchair at seven years of age.

But Tanni's determination to defy her disability has made her and her mean machine, a force to be reckoned with. This feisty politics graduate is popularly recognized as the fastest woman on three wheels in the world today.

Fresh from her morning training session she parks herself in the kitchen and with a cup of coffee muses over the accolade. "The fastest woman in the world? Over sprint distances I am pretty fast, but for me, the main thing is winning," she says. "I like winning and hate losing. Only winning drives me on to do things better next time."

The feature also highlighted how the media had identified Tanni as an articulate spokeswoman for her sport during and after the Barcelona Games.

"The press coverage in Barcelona outshone anything we had in Seoul," says Tanni. "It helped, I think, for people to see us as real athletes, not a novelty sport."

But Tanni is not easily fooled, she knows that a thirty minute slot on Grandstand every four years is not going to make disabled sport popular viewing.

Tanni's life off the track was also revealed. Except for her ground floor accommodation, few concessions have been made to Tanni's disability in the large, detached house she shares with her parents, her sister Sian and Chum the dog. At home Tanni is just Tanni. If something is out of reach, she just has to try harder.

That's the way Tanni likes things to be.

'When I was little I didn't realise I was disabled, all I knew was that I kept falling over a lot. I must have been about six or seven when Mum told me I had spina bifida and asked me what I was going to do about it.'

Isabel George's article identified what it described as a paradox in Tanni's life.

Was she the ideal role model for disabled children when she had always done her utmost to defy disability?

Nevertheless Tanni's achievements were used by many organizations to help promote particular initiatives for disabled people. Sometimes this was just a matter of Tanni endorsing an organization with her presence, but there were times when she helped put a greater weight behind a project by working for it directly. A good example of this was when she was sponsored by a major oil company to take part in its programme to encourage disabled youngsters into higher education.

She has also helped Contact, a voluntary organization for disabled people, by working on a series of local radio programmes and an accompanying booklet.

"I've always tried to steer clear of anything with a 'for the disabled' tag, in my bid to prove that disability is irrelevant when it comes to achievement. But now I am older and perhaps a little wiser, I recognize that people are only limited by their own perceptions of what they can do. This is a refreshing opportunity for me to help others who need to know what is available through education in sport – and be encouraged to go for it."

Tanni admitted to Isabel George that she hates getting up in the morning and hates the road, the treadmill and the swimming which are required for training.

'My disability is never going to go away so I don't see any point in hoping for a miracle cure. I can't get up and walk, and with my hunched body I don't think I would want to. So I have a wheelchair – so what – I'm still an athlete.'

Tanni receives the first bloom of the 'John Grooms' rose on behalf of the John Grooms Association.

Right: In 1993 Tanni becomes the youngest ever sports personality to be included in the Welsh Sports Hall of Fame.

Below: In the same year, Neil Kinnock interviews her on his television series 'Six of One'.

Below: The 'Children in Need' line-up. Terry Wogan introduces Tanni along with other top sports stars.

Left: A familiar sight around her home in Cardiff – Tanni out road training.

Right: John Harris and Tanni training at the athletics stadium in Cardiff.

Left: Behind the scenes things are often far from glamorous. Tanni shivering with fellow competitors after a race.

Left: Tanni covers up to 50 miles a day when training. Her carefully gloved hands show the wear that this involves.

Right: Victorious again. Tanni wins four gold medals at the World Championships in Berlin in 1994.

Below: Prince Charles was also in Australia in 1994 and presented Tanni with her award for second place in the Quantas Oz Day 10km road race in Sydney.

Far left: Tanni in her capacity as the English men's wheelchair team manager at the Commonwealth Games in Canada in 1994.

Left: With the mayor at the start of the Cardiff 10km race in 1994.

Below left: Tanni keeps up the pace at a charity push from Liverpool to Manchester.

Right: At home with Chum, the family dog.

Below: Helping with publicity for the launch of the RAC Disabled Driver of the Year in 1995.

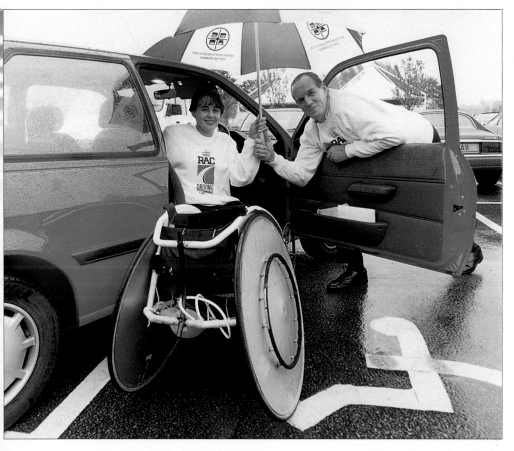

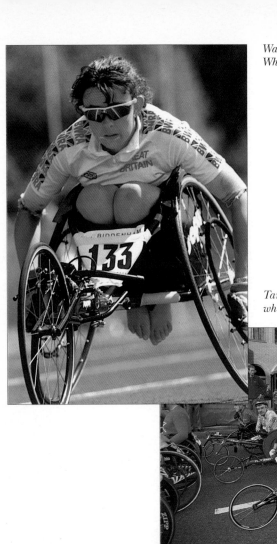

Warming up for the 1995 World
Wheelchair Games at Stoke Mandeville.

Tanni in the Great Midland Run 1995
which she went on to win.

The family together.

Once the post Paralympic season of 1993 was in full swing Tanni's international engagements kept her on the move. That summer, she lined up at the International Wheelchair Marathon in Heidelberg, Germany, coming home in fourth place behind the winner Connie Hansen from Denmark. And, as one of the athletes invited to the Canadian gathering, she went to Toronto for the Metro Toronto Wheelchair Challenge.

From Toronto she went back across the Atlantic for a race on 1 July in Denmark at the Arhus Games. A week after that she was the guest of honour invited to the award ceremony at the Fitzallen High School in Llandaff. The following day she and her parents drove to Loughborough for the ceremony in which she received her honorary Master of Arts degree.

In Britain, Tanni normally drives from event to event, able to take her day chair and racing chair in her car and to be entirely independent. On trips abroad though, she is in the hands of airlines and has become vastly experienced in the art of securing herself a trouble-free passage. This however often involves her in taking a firm line with meddling officialdom

She remembers one incident when she allowed the airport officials to take her day chair away from her when she checked in. She then had to rely on someone pushing her through the airport in an uncomfortable and badly designed airport chair and has never allowed this to happen again.

Now, at check-ins, Tanni flatly refuses to give her chair up. She is perfectly able to get herself to the plane gate and always leaves plenty of time for the airport authorities to get her on the plane and stow her chair away.

When officials try to get her into an airport chair, she starts off by being very polite and explaining patiently why she would prefer to remain in her own chair and then, if necessary, demands to see the airport manager. In the end, despite the rules, she is let through to avoid a public row.

'During such incidents,' she said, 'I try to remain calm because it doesn't do any good if I get mad and start screaming abuse. But there usually comes a point when I have to say "Look, I'm not going to be treated like an idiot". I am experienced enough now to know that if they think they can persuade me to do things their way, they will talk down to me. Sometimes I say with a smile "Yes, of course, you can have my chair," but then I add "provided you take everyone else's shoes and socks off at the check-in and make them walk through the airport in bare feet". That usually gets to them!

'Now that I am older, I do not put up with such attitudes to disability. I have a temper and I am bloody-minded, which I'm sure I get from my mum, so, these days, if I think I'm in the right about something, I argue.

'Similar problems arise getting off the plane. Officials say they'll help me off and push me through the airport, and I say I don't want to be pushed.

'Provided I have an aisle seat on the plane and my own chair for getting off the plane, I can handle my luggage, racing chair and kit, and seldom need an extra hand. I don't like being pushed and certainly don't want to be pushed through an airport. I suppose 'degrading' might be too strong a word for this but as a very fit athlete, it annoys me to think that they think I need to be pushed.

'There are some airports where restrictions on chairs are very strict. For example, in the United States, airport officials are aware that wheelchairs can be used for drug smuggling. When this is explained, I can see that there's a good reason why I should give up my chair and I am prepared to do so.

'In some airports where I've brought my racing chair to the gate they say "How d'you sit in this?". I say "I'm not going to sit in it now, that's my racing chair". And they then add "Well, can't you just go through the airport in it?". And I say "No, of course I can't, I'm not wearing the right clothes and I wouldn't fit into it". People find it hard to differentiate between someone who's old with a disability and someone who's disabled and yet is perfectly fit.

'I also have to take a lot of kit with me if I'm racing – the racing chair, two sets of wheels, tyres and a pump compressor. It's pretty heavy to cart around. I've also usually got a computer with me, my studies and my rucksack on my back. Then there are the bags of clothes. By and large, I can dump all this on a trolley and get through. Pushing the trolley is okay, but not easy. If I do need help there's usually airport staff around and I will ask for it.'

Because a racing wheelchair is an unusual item, Tanni often has to explain what it is that she is carrying. Likewise, although racing chairs are tough, they cannot take too much rough treatment and just be dumped on to a conveyor belt.

'I explain this to officials and they say things like, "Oh yes, I understand. My mother-in-law's got a wheelchair, and they're worth about £250, aren't they?". I say "Well, multiply that by ten and you might be a bit closer to what this one is worth". Again they're surprised. Explaining all this in a nice way works a lot better than having a go at them. The ignorance around is incredible, but it is getting better. I suppose it's the same for all sports people who have to carry their kit with them. I am just glad I am not a pole vaulter!'

Once Tanni's racing chair was damaged on a flight and since then for particularly important events, she has her chair boxed up to avoid a similar occurrence. So far, she has not been surcharged for extra luggage, but she knows Australian athletes who have been and hopes this will not happen to her one day.

Once in the air, even on the long-distance hauls, Tanni experiences very few problems. The air crew have access to aisle chairs for wheelchair-users but if she needs to go to the lavatory, she prefers to crawl along the aisle. This is quicker than waiting for someone to get the special aisle chair and put it up. She accepts that in doing this, she is conspicuous but argues that she is equally conspicuous if she has to wait to be taken in an aisle chair.

She knows that, for many passengers, she is an object of curiosity. When, in response to questions, she explains that she is an athlete some passengers reply 'Are you, dear? Oh, that's nice' and have no idea what to say next. However, since winning the London Marathon, she is often recognized for what she does, and says that, because it is televised, the London race carries more kudos with the public than the Barcelona Golds.

'They recognize me from the London Marathon, but don't know much about the Paralympic Games.'

On one flight to Australia, she was recognized by the person sitting next to her and enjoyed the glow that goes with public acknowledgement. On other occasions however she finds passengers inadvertently insulting. Having heard that she is an athlete, and having said 'How nice', they have been known to add 'At least, it means you can get out of the house and have an interest, doesn't it?'.

The ultimate insult meted out to Tanni by an airline, came in November of 1993. To take up her Churchill Travel Scholarship, Tanni had booked a Cathay Pacific flight to Australia and had paid £873 from her travel money for the journey. Then the airline told her that, because she used a wheelchair, they could not allow her to fly alone and that she would have to pay for someone to accompany her.

Later, speaking to the press, Tanni said: 'To say I am absolutely furious would be an understatement. I've flown all over the world by myself to compete, including New Zealand, the USA and Korea, without any problems and this has come something of a shock – especially as they cashed my cheque a month ago. There was even talk of me paying a ten per cent cancellation fee when I said I would try another airline, but that has been dropped.'

Unashamedly manipulating the media, Tanni pulled out all the stops to embarrass the airline.

'Even the booking form was offensive, asking if my disability would be likely to cause offence to other passengers.

'In the end I had the top European manager grovelling on the phone. He was terribly sorry, he said. But then he dug himself into an even deeper hole, saying that if he had realized the consequences in advance he would never, of course, have suggested that she could not travel alone. At that point I lost my temper. "Are you saying that you did it because you thought you could get away with it?"'

Tanni got a full refund from Cathay Pacific and when she eventually travelled to Australia, with British Airways, she was unaccompanied.

Although she expresses irritation with some people's condescending attitude towards wheelchair athletes, she is also prepared to defend them, saying that they do not realize how patronizing they are being. They are just not used to being around disabled people.

But to what lengths would Tanni go to support the political wing of the disability movement? Would she, for example, lie down in front of buses, as some disabled rights activists have been known to do in Whitehall? She answers that she is not into demonstrations and waving banners, but wants to tackle attitudes by showing people that she is not incapacitated or stupid.

'I get further by working with people rather than shouting at them,' she says. But she then admits that sometimes she has a good scream when she's on her own.

In general, she believes that the media now shows her sport in a more positive light than it did in the past and that able-bodied people are now talking about wheelchair athletes as achievers rather than, to use her own phrase as, 'disabled people having a go'.

Rather than the view that many outsiders have of the amateur nature of wheelchair racing, Tanni must, in order to remain at the top of her profession, keep up-to-date with the latest wheelchair technology and as a top-rank athlete she has become involved in negotiating sponsorship deals. Although these deals are not in the same league as those attracted by Linford Christie and others, Tanni is nevertheless ahead of almost everyone else in the Paralympic field. She is, sponsors know, a bankable commodity. If Tanni can be seen to be using their products and endorsing their marketing campaigns, they will benefit.

For commercial public appearances, Tanni receives fees of between £100–£300. Other money, sponsorship deals and media appearances are handled by her solicitors, Morgan Bruce.

There is far more money now in disabled sport than ever before, especially in the United States. The winner of the Boston Marathon for example can earn up to $30,000 if a world record is broken. Not surprisingly this has resulted in an element of gamesmanship bordering on cheating, in which disabled athletes have attempted to fool the classifiers and get themselves into an easier category. This does not of course apply in open events where the major prize money can be won, but in competitions where classifications make an important difference, the less scrupulous can have an advantage.

When a deal comes along which Tanni believes could produce some 'real money' then solicitor Bleddyn Rees from Morgan Bruce becomes involved. He, Tanni believes, has got the guts to ask for more than she would ever dare. For example, a television appearance that Tanni might be happy to do for £50, is negotiated at £1,000 when Bleddyn is on the case. In the end, a fee is usually agreed somewhere below that figure but considerably above the £50 that Tanni would have accepted.

She is also assisted by the Sports Council for Wales, which helps in 'marrying' athletes and businesses in commercial sponsorship deals.

For Tanni, an agreement made with the business consultants and accountants, Price Waterhouse Wales, is worth £2,000. In return, she wears the Price Waterhouse logo on her hat and her chair, and occasionally puts in appearances at company-sponsored functions.

Tanni also uses branded equipment through the firm Sunrise Medical. She is the only athlete in the country who is paid to race by a chair company.

At the time of the Barcelona Games she was using a Bromakin chair, but later accepted a sponsorship offer from Top End and later still, moved on to Sunrise Medical. Moving from one chair company to another is always a difficult decision for her, but Sunrise Medical make chairs specifically for her at their factory in Germany, and all Tanni needs to do is visit the factory from time to time to supervise the work.

'I pick up a chair, check it is okay, take it away, get a few things altered, send it back for some other things to be fixed and in the end get the chair that is really right.'

Following an unfortunate experience with Top End, Tanni had been ripe for the sponsorship approach which came from Sunrise Medical. During her second year with Top End she had become unhappy, feeling she was rather isolated from the company's plans and long-term strategic thinking. The firm had also changed hands and was under new management. Then, at the Naidex exhibition in London, the exhibition of equipment and services for disabled people, Tanni found herself at the Top End stand.

'One of the marketing managers tried to sell me my own racing chair! He just came up to me and asked if I was interested in Top End chairs. I was saying "Oh, yes, sure I am", thinking that he was having a laugh when he said "Have you ever tried racing? Maybe you should give it a go."

Tanni, still thinking he was joking, played along for a few minutes, but then she realized he was not joking, and was indeed trying to sell her a racing chair and encourage her to take part in the sport. Eventually one of the other athletes came up and said to him, 'I don't think you really want to be selling Tanni Grey a racing chair' and the salesman said 'Why not?' The athlete replied, 'Well, she's already got four Gold medals from the Paralympics for track racing'.

The man's face fell in horror and embarrassment. As amusing as the unfortunate incident was, it led Tanni to think that Top End were not as truly interested in her racing career as they might have been. She also began to have doubts about whether they could guarantee further sponsorship until the Atlanta Games, especially when another of the marketing team kept asking her when she was going to retire from racing. She did not feel this was the most positive of approaches.

Then, out of the blue, she received a timely telephone call from Sunrise Medical asking if she would be interested in a sponsorship deal with them and negotiations began.

'I felt they had a good British base. They were moving into the racing chair side, were sponsoring athletes and were into a lot of publicity. I felt I had more of a chance with them and it's been a good arrangement. But it wasn't easy breaking the news to Top End.'

The company actually took the news very well and even asked if they could give her a better deal. Tanni however was not interested in playing the two companies off against each other, she just wanted definite offers to compare. It was then hinted that Top End were going to offer her a job in their marketing department – an added encouragement to stay with them perhaps?

'How they knew I'd be the right person for that job when they didn't even know my educational background, I don't know.'

She had actually made the decision to join Sunrise Medical but was pleased that she had left Top End on reasonably amicable terms and that they had indicated that the door was open for her to return if she wished.

'It was one of the hardest things for me to do,' Tanni recalls. 'Just after I moved, I went out to compete in the Boston marathon. At the airport I met the man who used to own Top End. It was an awkward meeting because he and his wife were really very nice people. I'm not sure he really understood my reasons and I don't know whether he felt he'd been stabbed in the back. I didn't want to hurt them. But once the original owner had sold Top End, it wasn't his business any more and, with him in a different capacity, I didn't feel things were the same.'

Tanni's contract with Sunrise Medical is an important support for her racing programme. Travelling to and from events however is her responsibility, although she receives money from many different sources depending on who she is competing for. Most competitions however also involve her in paying something herself.

The deal with Price Waterhouse Wales was announced at the end of March 1994 and was described as a sponsorship arrangement to help Tanni through the build-up to the Berlin

World Championships in the summer. It was designed to help her pay for travel and accommodation to the United States where she would be spending much of the spring. The funding was most welcome because ahead of her were marathons in London and Switzerland, as well as a string of competitions over shorter distances.

At the time, Derek Howell, from Price Waterhouse Wales, said, 'Tanni is an extremely talented athlete who has already achieved outstanding success as an all-rounder. We believe, given the backing she needs, that she has the ability to achieve even greater success. We hope our backing will help her to realize her full potential and ambition. All in all, she is a great prospect and we are delighted to be associated with the very best.'

This sponsorship deal paid off within three weeks of its announcement when Tanni crossed the line ahead of the field in the women's wheelchair section of the London Marathon. Lily Anggreny from Germany, who would have been a serious contender, had pulled out of the event on the Friday through illness.and so on this occasion, Tanni was not up against the same overseas competition of previous years and her overall time of 2 hours 8 minutes and 26 seconds was 18 minutes outside her best.

Nevertheless, her delighted sponsors published a photograph of her in an advertisement in the *Western Mail* 'Business Week', making full use of its association with a winner.

For Tanni, this was yet another major trophy to add to her collection and she received a first prize of £1,000, and registered her second win. Rose Hill, who had defeated her the year before, found that form was favouring Tanni. It was however a close tussle and Tanni's tactics of staying with her rival until the very end and then beating her on a sprint finish paid off. Rose was beaten at the last minute by a mere four seconds. Despite the disappointing time, Tanni described the marathon afterwards as one of her best.

'I knew that if I was still with Rose at twenty miles then I had a good chance. In the closing yards, it's as much psychological as anything.'

Alix Ramsey reporting on the race in *The Times* said:

*Just as two years ago, when Grey last won in London, neither she
nor Hill was willing to take the lead over the last mile and a half,
Hill fearing Grey's speed and Grey not wanting to push the pace
from too far out.*

*After a winter of warm weather training in Australia and stints
on the American road racing circuit, Grey's stamina and road
fitness is better than last year, when she finished third. With the
World Championships on the horizon she is planning to race every
distance from 100 metres to 10,000 metres, with two more
marathons planned in Switzerland and Berlin.*

As well as attention in the press, the BBC television documentary
on Tanni had been shown on 14 April 1994 as a preview to the
London Marathon. It showed Tanni training and competing,
and included some black-and-white archive footage of the early
Paralympians in their baggy vests and sturdy chairs.

Tanni comments on how odd it was to see a programme about
herself.

'It was a very strange feeling watching the finished programme, seeing how I was viewed by other perople. It was the first
time a programme like this had been made about me and I
learned a lot about myself.'

CHAPTER SEVEN

Achievements and dilemmas

*It is hard to believe that the world's fastest woman
on the three wheels has been temporarily grounded
by a cup of coffee.*
Sally Jones, The Observer

FOR TANNI THE key event of the 1993 season was the fourth
World Athletics Championships in Stuttgart, Germany, an international meeting regarded by many athletes as almost on a par
with the Olympic Games. The 800-metres wheelchair race for
women was one of the Paralympic sports included as an
exhibition event. Tanni, racing in Lane 1, wearing 995, was the
only T3 in the race which was won by the Australian Louise
Sauvage, 6 seconds ahead of Connie Hansen of Denmark. Tanni
was hot on Connie's heels crossing the line in 2 minutes 1.22
seconds in Bronze medal position.

The next month Tanni was in Denmark competing in the
5000, 2000, 1500, 400, 100 metres and 10 km races in a space of a
couple of days. Later she went to Monte Carlo, not to race but for
the session of the International Olympic Committee which was
to determine the location of the Olympic Games in the year
2000.

Tanni had worked hard to promote the eventually unsuccessful Manchester bid for the games in the year 2000.

In many ways it was important for the Paralympic movement
to secure a bid in a country where the attitudes towards disability
sports were well developed and the facilities adequate-to-good.
Atlanta, which is to host the 1996 games, was by that time causing

concern because of disagreement about whether athletes with learning difficulties should be included in the full Paralympic Games. Little progress, too, had been made on the inclusion of exhibition- or medal-status disability sports in the full Olympic Games.

Athletes, such as Tanni were steadily becoming more influential on the policy side. If they, through the British Paralympic movement, could have secured the Games for Britain in the year 2000, they would have had a substantial say in the way the Paralympic Games were viewed, promoted and financed.

Then abruptly, thanks to a cup of coffee, Tanni's globe-trotting came to an end that autumn. The scalding drink, spilt over Tanni's legs, damaged the skin so seriously that Tanni had to be hospitalized in the burns unit at Chepstow.

Writing in *The Observer* in October, Sally Jones said:

Watching Tanni Grey's vivid elfin face transformed by the range of emotions flitting across it, from frustration to wild joy, it is hard to believe that the world's fastest woman on the three wheels has been temporarily grounded by a cup of coffee.

The scalding of her legs was a very serious incident for Tanni because poor circulation below her waist means that wounds are very slow to heal. When the accident happened, she was at Ian Thompson's home at Redcar, having just taken part in the Great North Run and now preparing for the annual Batley 10-km event.

She was sitting on the edge of her seat, wearing thin Lycra trousers and holding a cup, when her leg had an involuntary spasm, causing her to fall back in her chair, spilling the hot coffee over herself. Although she felt no pain, her leg immediately went into hyper-spasm. She took her trousers off, splashed cold water over her leg, filled a bath with cold water, lay in it and began to feel very cold. She resisted Ian's offer to call an ambulance and only agreed when she realized that the skin was blistering and falling off in chunks.

She was taken to the local casualty department and in due course, after some administrative hassle, was transferred to the burns unit at Chepstow. Such was the concern over the effect of the scald that, in the early stages, all visitors needed to be masked and gowned to prevent cross-infection.

Hospitalization meant that her training schedule had to be put on ice and, for a while, her overseas Churchill Scholarship trip was in jeopardy. Even in hospital, Tanni was determined to continue her training as much as possible. And to do this she kept a set of dumbbells under her hospital bed, using these to maintain her upper body strength with weight-lifting routines. She also asked her parents to bring in a static hand-bike.

'From the moment I got to Chepstow my legs began to improve,' she said.

Shortly before her hospitalization, Tanni had been one of Neil Kinnock's guests on *Six of the Best*, a chat show which the former Labour leader recorded for BBC Wales. As usual she said her piece, coming out with some memorable quotes, particularly on the subject of education.

Warming to her favourite theme, she told Neil Kinnock, 'The shame is that people look at people like me, see that we haven't got the use of our legs and then think that we are in need of special education. But the truth is that there are a lot of kids walking around who would actually benefit from special education but who do not get it because they can walk.'

Fortunately for Tanni, her scald mended well and the feared plastic surgery was not required. She was able to leave Chepstow and look forward to her Australian visit.

By November, Tanni's competitions for the following summer were taking shape. The dates of all the major events had been fixed and her diary was filling up fast. Most of the engagements were accepted without much discussion – but Tanni received one attractive proposition that caused her something of a dilemma. During the winter of 1994, Lillehammer in Norway was hosting the Winter Olympic Games. Not, one might suppose, a matter of great interest to Tanni, except that, for a short while, she was tempted by the idea of taking up speed-skating so that she could include the Winter Games in her schedule. This would have required adapting techniques but doubtless her competitive skills and tactical mind would have put her in line for a medal -or so the selectors of the speed-skating squad believed. In the end however she turned the offer down.

'If I had had two years training on the right equipment I would have been ready, but I hadn't. I would have loved to have been there representing Britain – but I don't think it would have been fair to myself or the team if I went. I like to win. I am used to winning and would not have liked to go there and lose. Maybe that's arrogant but unless I am in a position to give my best I don't think it's right for me to take part.'

In a November interview with Jeremy Bacon in the *Daily Telegraph*, Tanni announced that she would not be pursuing winter glory and took the opportunity to reinforce her message about disability sport. She related the story of how when she returned from the Paralympic Games in Spain, a journalist had come up to her and asked if she trained. He clearly thought that she had just turned up in Barcelona and had a go.

'When Linford Christie and Sally Gunnell returned from the Games no-one asked them such an insulting question' Tanni said. 'That sort of attitude, epitomized by the journalists, really annoys me because it devalues the whole Paralympic movement. Unfortunately, many people cannot look beyond the wheel-chair. No matter how many times you tell them a racing chair is a piece of sporting equipment like Steve Backley's javelin, they still respond with the patronizing attitude about how brave and wonderful you are.'

Underlying Tanni's decision not to go to Lillehammer was undoubtedly the idea that she was not the type of person to just turn up and have a go for the fun of it. She was an elite competitor in her own field and in her own right. In her eyes it would devalue the Paralympic movement if she turned up at Lillehammer just for the fun of it, unprepared. It was only because of a desire to extend and improve her training methods for her wheelchair-racing that she had even contemplated joining one of the winter Olympic squads. She left the question of future winter games open however, thinking that perhaps in four years time she might have time to train for and take up a winter sports event.

But first there was Australia, where Tanni had the chance to team up and train with Louise Sauvage, another of the world's elite. This involved two months away under the coaching of Jenny Banks in the Western Australian sun.

Louise found working with Tanni a great advantage because normally she trained with men whose greater strength meant that she was always chasing, never leading the pack. The two athletes were number one in their own class. Louise, a T4, had won three Gold medals at the sprint distances in the Paralympics. Both she and Tanni had competed in a number of prestigious marathons.

The trip to Australia was financed by the Churchill Scholarship for the trustees of which, as well as training, Tanni was expected to write a report on what she had learned from her experience. Originally she had hoped to go to Illinois, the Mecca so to speak of women's wheelchair-racing in the United States, and had been awarded a scholarship to work in Canada and the United States. When she discovered that she could not go to Illinois unless she went for a whole year, she decided to go to Australia instead. Once there, she stayed with Louise Sauvage and, having got to know leading coach Jenny Banks at the Stuttgart World Games in 1993, began to train with her.

'Australia is far better than Britian at co-ordinating disability training between the different groups', Tanni explains. 'There is also more coverage of wheelchair sport in the press and events are better intergrated into the able-bodied track and field programme. Also in three-and-a-half months of my stay in Australia, it only rained for three minutes!'

Tanni's visit to Australia coincided with the visit of the Prince of Wales and, after she had taken part in the Qantas Oz Day 10km race, he presented her with a medal for coming in second place. It was during this visit that Prince Charles boosted his tarnished image by retaining his cool when a man lunged at him with a starting pistol. Tanni however saw none of this excitement.

The 10 km race was described as the world's top showdown for disabled athletes. The course in Sydney was to pass the Opera House and the historic Rocks area and go under the Harbour Bridge.

Western Australian Louise Sauvage, described by a partisan Australian press as 'by far the best female wheelchair athlete in the world', was quoted as saying that she wanted to show Australia what she could do. She was confident of retaining her crown.

Louise Sauvage, although four years younger than Tanni, is her Australian equivalent. She plays down her position as a role-model for disabled children who need heroes, and emphasizes instead her position as an elite athlete, achieving what she does through hard work and training.

'But I do try to show others that if you want success badly enough you can, with a lot of dedication and sacrifice, achieve it,' she added.

Jenny Banks talked the sport up as a spectator event that people would want to watch. All good hype!

'Quite frankly,' Jenny admitted, 'I would rather watch the Paralympic athletes than the Olympians. Able-bodied athletics is not half as exciting.'

Tanni flew back to England in February and after just two weeks at home was on the move again. This time, clutching her boarding pass and manoeuvring her kit and chair at Gatwick airport, she was en route to the United States to compete in the Los Angeles Marathon. Once there, she recorded a time of 1 hour 54 minutes and 40 seconds, and an overall place of twenty-first, making her the third fastest woman. She also went in for a 10 km race and flew to Florida for the Gasparilla Distance Classic.

At the end of 1993, Tanni's track records had received what many would accept to be the ultimate acknowledgement – an entry in the 1994 edition of the *Guinness Book of Records*. Page 282 showed a photograph of Tanni with the caption:

One of the most successful participants in the 1992 Paralympics in Barcelona was Tanni Grey (GB) who won four golds, wheelchair records for 100, 200, 400 and 800 metres and British records for 1500, 500 metres, half and full marathon distances.

Writing to Peter Grey in February 1994, the editor of the *Guinness Book of Records*, Peter Matthews, said that he was planning to extend the Paralympic records in the next edition. He wanted to include a series of wheelchair world records for both men and women. He admitted that other reference books on sport which he edited, *The International Who's Who of Sport* and *The Guinness Encyclopedia of International Sports Records and Results,* did not include details of Paralympic events. Giving his reasons for this he put most succinctly the problem faced by many commentators and reporters in raising interest in the sport. Wheelchair records, he said, were about the only Paralympic activities easy for him to include in the *Guinness Book of Records.*

'We have to concentrate on records which are not qualified, other than splitting into men and women. Thus we are not able to include specific age records and, going further, nor are we able to include records qualified by some particular physical disability. The Paralympics is sub-divided into huge numbers of categories and it simply would not be practical for us to be able to include records in all such categories. That's why wheelchair records are great to include, because they could indeed be open to fully able-bodied people as well as for people with different degrees of disability.'

In a nutshell, the sports dilemma, as outlined by an outsider. Spectators could grasp what was involved with elite wheelchair-racing and concentrate on certain personalities, but when it came to all the other categories and events the interest waned considerably.

The London Marathon presented a good example of this. While it is only one of many annual events for Paralympic athletes, it is the one which receives the greatest public recognition because it involves the wheelchair elite.

In the middle of April, Tanni found herself once again on the starting line in Blackheath. Two years before, in favourable circumstances, she had won. The year before, she had lost her title. Now in 1994 she defeated Rose Hill in a very tight finish with a time of 2 hours, 8 minutes and 26 seconds, proving herself both as a marathon competitor and, in the final stages, as a sprinter.

When asked by *The Independent*'s sports writer, Duncan Mackay, about her versatility, she replied:

'It's not versatility, it's stupidity. Even though the distances appear so different, you have to do high-mileage training for sprinting so it's not that hard to do the marathon. Unlike running, it's about momentum not gravity.'

The weather conditions were not good. It was in fact very cold but Tanni saw the positive side of this as it made her fingers so numb after about a mile that it helped to take the pain away.

'London's road surfaces were of more concern to the wheelchair-racers.' she said. 'Every time they hit a pot-hole, the impact sent a shudder through their bodies; and the padding over the cobbles at the Tower of London were not so much a magic carpet ride as a trip to hell. It was worst for me because, at seven stone, I'm so light I don't travel well over the surface and after a while everything hurt – especially my neck.'

The month finished with Tanni taking part in the British Wheelchair Association Track Championships at Leicester. In two days she took part in seven races, including the 10,000 metres which she won in 27 minutes 37.7 seconds.

On 6 May, Tanni was at the Guildhall in London where the Speaker, Betty Boothroyd, was the guest of honour at the presentation of the 1994 Winston Churchill Memorial Trust medallions. Others receiving medallions had studied subjects as diverse as wind farms, sign writing, jazz education, contemporary jewellery and women in the prison system, to name just a few of the hugely diverse range of subjects.

After grand events, one always finds less grand but just as worthwhile events in Tanni's diary. Shortly after the Guildhall presentation in all the glitter of the city's most prestigious building, Tanni was in Colchester for the Disability Sport's Forum Committee Festival day. There, she lent encouragement and gave advice to around 1000 disabled people from the East Anglia area who had come to Colchester's Leisure World to try out various sports for themselves.

One price of celebrity status is that the press can sometimes embarrass you by catching you out. At the end of May, the *South Wales Echo* decided to run a short quiz about the European election. The questions included: Who is the local Euro MP? What date is the Euro election? Where do the members sit? As well as putting these question to readers and local politicians, the paper also selected five sportsmen and women. Caught unawares, politics graduate Tanni admitted that she had not a clue as to who her MEP was; thought that the elections were to take place some time in the next couple of weeks, and added: 'I studied European politics for a year and know nothing about it. It was boring.' She then guessed correctly that Strasbourg is where the members would be sitting.

The next invitation sent to Tanni was for an evening reception on 20 June at Buckingham Palace where, according to the Court Circular, Prince Edward, Princess Anne, Princess Margaret and various other members of the royal family were to be present. It was said the detailed instructions from Buckingham Palace, a black-tie formal occasion although lounge suit for gentlemen would be equally in order.

As with any royal occasion, this was a glittering evening – literally in that the surroundings were gilt, the lighting was by chandelier and some of the greatest works of art were on the wall. By now Tanni, who had met members of the royal family on many occasions before, was well used to such occasions. At the reception, she also saw lots of other people she had seen previously on the royal circuit. It is one of the paradoxes of the British system which so loves to honour those who have achieved that, lauded as Tanni now was by the wealthy establishment, she still had problems which could so easily have been resolved if only some of that wealth had been redirected.

Just a few days before this wealthy, glittering, royal event, it had been suggested to Tanni that she might have to pay her own way when she took part in July's World Disabled Athletics Championships in Berlin. The World Championships were the highlight of the season and Tanni was determined to take part. But the event, although almost as important as the Olympics to the elite athletes, had none of the public appeal of a Paralympic year. The British Paralympic Association was short of funds and the costs for each athlete to go to Berlin were estimated at £800.

In June she told the *South Wales Echo* 'In the past we have always had help with our costs (for international events), but on this occasion it looks as if we'll have to try and fund ourselves. I'm quite fortunate in that I already have sponsorship, but this situation will mean I will have to cut down on some of my preparatory races. At least I haven't got to travel too far to compete. Some of the Australian team will be looking at costs of about A$5,000.'

The BPA had already had to fund the winter Paralympic team and it is Tanni's insight into and understanding of these internal problems that have turned her into an athlete who is very much aware of the organizational problems of her sport. Conscious that much change needs to take place, she is formulating various proposals and suggestions that she will incorporate into her masters degree thesis on the politics of disability sport. She first considered pursuing a postgraduate degree back in 1992 and is now registered through the Cardiff Institute of Higher Education for a University of Wales degree studying for a Master of Philosophy. She hopes to have completed it on a part-time basis by 1998.

'I was not only interested in exploring the issues,' she explains over her motives for studying for a further degree, 'but it also seemed a good preparation for some of the possible directions my future career might take.'

As far as the World Disabled Athletics Championships were concerned, on this occasion, in the nick of time, the British team to Berlin was saved. The Foundation for Sport and the Arts came to its rescue with a grant of £20,000. Thanks to this, the squad of eighty-one athletes, for which the BPA were only able to raise the £36,000 to pay the team's entrance fee, did not have to be sacrificed. An additional £10,000 was also donated by various disability associations, including the British Wheelchair Racing Association which was also sending athletes to the Championships.

The only athletes not taking part were three with learning difficulties who had failed to meet the required standard laid down by the organizers. However, seven other athletes with learning disabilities were to take part in the Games. This decision to allow a small degree of integration between the Paralympic movement and athletes with learning difficulties came at a time when the disagreement threatening the Atlanta Paralympics of 1996 was coming to a head.

After the Barcelona Games, in which no athletes with learning difficulties were included (they had had their own games in Madrid shortly afterwards) a statement was made that the two games would be amalgamated next time. Athletes, including Tanni, had grave reservations about this integration. In July 1994 Tanni was quoted in the *Daily Telegraph* as saying that the issue was threatening to destroy the hard-won public relations achievement of disabled athletes in recent years. Her concern centres around the way disability sport is moving on rather than questioning the standard of the athletes:

'There are many with learning difficulties that are good athletes – it is just the context and the way that they compete that I have concerns about.'

Ian Thompson was also quoted as saying that, when the Paralympic athletes had been told about the integration, they could not believe it. He estimated that up to ninety percent of physically disabled athletes were against bringing the two groups together.

It remains an issue that threatens to divide the Paralympic movement and it is no exaggeration to suggest that it could undermine or even destroy much of the progress that has been made over the last eight years. This progress has involved wheelchair athletes, especially the elite, being accepted as sportsmen and sportswomen in their own right who can provide a first-class spectacle sport for everyone to enjoy. The fear is that, once athletes with learning difficulties or mental handicaps (depending on the terminology used) are included, the Games will again be perceived as 'unfortunate cripples doing their best'.

Of course a classification system can be devised to cope with this problem and separate the elite from the 'have-a-gos', but the fear of many Paralympic athletes is that, too often in society, people assume that a person with a physical disability also has a learning difficulty. For years, wheelchair-users have fought against the 'does he take sugar?' syndrome in which it is taken for granted that people with physical disabilities are unable to have opinions, or express themselves.

Nobody denies that, unless helped by skilled advocates, many disabled people with learning difficulties are not able to form opinions and express them. The point is that people with learning difficulties have a different type of disability from those with some form of physical impairment.

Bernard Ather however, a member of the International Paralympic Committee who has championed the progress of mentally-disabled athletes, believes that, in terms of public attitude, it is prejudice and discrimination to separate the two groups of athletes.

'When people think of athletes with learning difficulties, they see happy smiling faces, the 'everyone's a winner' idea. Some of these athletes however are of extremely high calibre.'

He cites the British sprinter Kenny Colaine MBE, who won Gold in the 100 and 200 metres in the Madrid Games and was voted Athlete of the Year in his field.

'We don't want war over this,' Bernard Ather said in a *Sunday Telegraph* interview in July 1994, 'but the time will come when we have to make a stand.'

Tanni tends to see the dispute as another example of the separation that exists between administrators and athletes.

There might, she feels, have been a resolution to the problem but the athletes were angered by the sudden decision to amalgamate the two events, made directly after the Paralympic Games in Barcelona, without any consultation with the athletes who had taken part.

Tanni sees the Paralympics as an elite competition. The Paralympic movement, she believes, must safeguard this ideal. It has to enable cerebral palsy sports, and sports for people with visual impairment, to be played at an elite level.

One problem however is that in some events, and some classifications, there are not enough people who have reached the elite status that enables them to compete at the very highest level. One solution to this would be to cut back on the classifications and the events in the Paralympic Games, but here again lies a difficulty.

'We have to safeguard against people with severe disabilities being pushed out of the Paralympics because that could happen. It could mean that wheelchair competitors with nice straight bodies, who are normal size and speak well, would be the only people to be seen. People with more severe disabilities who are not as aesthetically pleasing might not be required in the new spectator sport.'

What Tanni believes has to happen is that more sport for disabled people should be encouraged at grass roots level so that more elite competitors can come through.

'There are difficulties because this is a young movement, started in a particular way to provide therapy for able-bodied people who had become disabled.

'If I could start everything from scratch, I would begin with a careful monitoring of children with disabilities in mainstream schools to ensure that they get physical education. One of the main problems with special schools is that they do not provide good enough PE – they provide good medical care, but not sporting opportunities.

'Even in mainstream education, the teachers do not have the experience or the time to devise special programmes for disabled children when there are thirty-five other children running around in the gymnasium for an hour.

'Physical education is particularly important for disabled children because it keeps them fit, and fit people don't get sick so often. I have certainly had fewer urinary tract infections since I've been as fit as I am. It is also essential for children in wheelchairs to be strong because they need to be able to transfer themselves from chair to chair and to crawl up and down stairs and so on. Encouraging this sort of thing is simply not happening.

'One of the problems may be that the medical profession has too low an expectation of people with disabilities. So what we are talking about is a complete change of attitude in society as a whole.

'I know it sounds as if I want to change the world – and I suppose I do – but I want to make changes so that children can get access to sport and find which sport they can excel at. Inevitably, some of these children will aim to compete at an elite level and would then provide competitors, even for some of the classifications which are traditionally less well filled.'

Because there are so many different types of disability and no way that a single PE teacher could have knowledge of them all, Tanni proposes developing further the system of PE advisers able to go around schools to ensure that disabled children are, as much as possible, integrated in physical education lessons. Where there cannot be simple integration, because of the disability or lack of facilities at the school, an adviser could then be on hand to suggest an alternative approach.

'I cannot propose that everyone in a wheelchair should have the right to take part in every event – being hit by a wheelchair in a football match would be pretty painful! Likewise, if kids have brittle bones, they can't do gymnastics. Children with Downs' Syndrome can't do roly-polies in case they damage their necks. There are lots of dos and don'ts, which is why special advisers could help PE teachers find just the right approach for individual children.'

Starting at school level, Tanni believes, would help change people's attitude towards disability sport.

'If you look at places, like Australia or America, they now have really good wheelchair athletes coming through at eleven and twelve years old. And, in two or three years time, I will have problems competing against them because they will have been racing since they were seven or eight years old. In Britain, at the moment, we don't really have such athletes until they are sixteen or seventeen.'

Tanni is extremely involved in encouraging people to take up sport. And she has found at Wheelchair Racing Association weekends that, when young people are introduced to sport, these are often the first occasions when they have experienced independence.

'We have twelve- and thirteen-year-olds coming to a residential weekend at Stoke Mandeville to learn about sport. And when they get up in the morning, we find that some of them don't know how to brush their teeth or have a shower because it's always been done for them. They have never been taught to manage for themselves at school or at home. When it comes to going up and down steps, it doesn't occur to them to get out of the chair and pull the chair up, even if they're able to. They have low expectations which they have been given by parents and others involved in their education. Everything is done for them.

'It does them no good because when they do come away, they worry about who's going to wash them or put their socks on. The additional problem is that many top athletes who have become disabled as a result of an accident and haven't been born with disabilities find such children hard to cope with.

'Some of the disabled children I see are really spoilt brats. One lad at a junior training week wouldn't even brush his own hair. "Mum always does it", he said. Sian was helping out and she's a bit like me. "Well,' she said to this lad, 'I'm not doing it for you. You'll have to do it yourself". And he said "But I've never done it before". You have to be patient because it's not their fault that they're like that.'

These training weekends, organized by the Wheelchair Racing Association at Stoke Mandeville, are open to anybody who is interested in wheelchair-racing and wants to try the sport. There are up to ten such weekends every year and getting to most of them has become a regular part of Tanni's round of engagements. The potential athletes arrive on Friday nights and stay until Sunday afternoon.

'They're very good occasions, like social weekends, with excellent training, a nice atmosphere and first-rate competition. People arrive aged between twelve and sixty years old, although the average age is around twenty-five to thirty.

'At junior weekends, we get much younger children because we try as far as possible to encourage parents to let the children come away on their own unless there are medical reasons for someone to be in attendance and we don't have the medical staff to cope. It really is good for them to be away from their parents for a while and it's good for the parents to have a break.'

Through taking part in these weekends, Tanni has noticed one or two promising athletes, but nothing like as promising as some she has seen in Australia and America. Sometimes there simply is not the necessary support at home, the funds to help travel or even the belief that an individual child can be both independent and an achiever.

She is looking ahead to the Paralympics of the year 2000, whatever form they take. But fears that, by then, she will be on the verge of retirement as will others like Rose Hill and Tracey Lewis. Tanni thinks that Britain could do badly in the medals' table as there are not the necessary newcomers emerging.

Perhaps this situation will come to change as Tanni's high profile encourages other children with disabilities to be determined enough to argue the toss with their parents. Hopefully their parents will let them gain the independence that Tanni experienced as a child. Tanni, too, might be able to encourage parents to allow their disabled children to aim at goals which in the normal course of events they might consider unattainable.

Rose Hill feels however that more could be done by the elite competitors themselves working as a team to promote excellence in their sport. She is particularly concerned that she and Tanni do not take advantage of training with each other. Yet Tanni is quick to point out that this would be very difficult in practise as they live over 100 miles apart and both follow very busy and very different schedules. Even so, Rose feels that together they could do more to encourage other disabled women to take up the sport. She is saddened that she and Tanni do not work more as a partnership.

There is a detectable friction in the rivalry between Tanni and Rose. They seldom travel to events together and Rose believes this is because: 'Tanni likes it all her own way and enjoys being the star'. Tanni however points out that few athletes travel together unless they are going as a team to a major event.

Overall, Rose and Tanni are in agreement that they want to see more men and women taking part in the sport and providing new and more challenging competition.

Rose does not, she says, speak from envy in that perhaps Tanni has eclipsed her achievements by taking the glory. She is fifteen years older than Tanni, has a family and took up racing after two years in a wheelchair following an accident which left her paralysed.

Rose is not one of what she perceives as the 'inner clique' of elite athletes, and has many other interests and commitments.

'I have no problems with Tanni taking on the role of ambassador for the sport. I am happy about that. I'm only competitive on the track. Away from it, I just want to have fun.'

Tanni admits that she and Rose do not get on particularly well and that the team spirit is not particularly thriving. Given that between them they make up the main part of the women's squad, this is hardly surprising. Tanni then confesses that both she and Rose are strong-minded and that it is probably this which makes both of them winners.

In reviewing the problems faced by the Paralympic movement, and especially the sport for disabled people in

Britain, Tanni also identifies an organizational fragmentation that creates many difficulties.

'We have too many governing bodies and no single development programme. The British Sports Association for the Disabled has a huge number of wheelchair athletes which the British Wheelchair Racing Association never sees because we don't work together. This is a real shame because a lot of people are losing out. The BSAD tends to be more recreational and the BWRA, of which I am a member, tends to be more serious about its athletics.

'There's also the British Wheelchair Athletics Association which the BWRA broke away from in 1989 for political reasons concerning the pentathletes. Now however they are working closely together again. The Cerebral Palsy sports body has a section of wheelchair racers; the British Paralympic Athletics Federation thinks of itself as the governing body for disabled athletes; and there is the British Paralympic Association.

'Standards and classifications however are overseen by the International Stoke Mandeville Wheelchair Sports Federation and the International Paralympic Committee is also involved in setting standards.'

'Thus there is a confusing array of governing bodies and no coherent link-up with able-bodied athletics clubs. I would like to see disabled sport and able-bodied sport linked together much more. From my experience, I've found it very useful to train with able-bodied people. I would certainly rather be a member of a mainstream sports club, with maybe one or two disabled participants, than a member of a disabled sporting group.'

When Chris Hallam reviews the current state of his sport, he cannot help but wonder if the Paralympic movement did not peak at Barcelona.

'It has all become very political now. The future looks topsy-turvy. The problem is internal, and there are conflicts between the disability groups. I personally feel that I have seen the best years of wheelchair-racing. Although, in saying that, I hope I haven't.'

Previously sympathetic with Tanni's idea that wheelchair-racing could become a sport open to all – able-bodied and disabled people alike – he now has some reservations.

'The trouble is that if able-bodied people take over they could squeeze out the athletes with disabilities. This could certainly happen if the numbers involved explode. There are obviously disadvantages in being disabled, even in wheelchair-racing. I never used to think like this, but I do now.'

Ian Thompson takes a middle view. He wants to see more evidence that able-bodied people have an advantage before taking a firm line on keeping wheelchair-racing an exclusive sport for disabled athletes. Chris, reviewing the Paralympic movement as a whole, appreciates that, in some sports and classifications, there are too few competitors to create an elite.

'In men's wheelchair-racing there is a pyramid structure. In Britain there are at least 250 serious racers and the elite are at the top of the pyramid. Some sports don't have the numbers to make up the pyramid required, so even if an outstanding individual emerges, he or she has no competition.'

In past Paralympics, Tanni believes it was too easy for competitors in some events to win international status.

'Just because people with disabilities play a sport, it doesn't give them an automatic right to represent their country,' she says. 'Because there are so many classifications, it was easy in the past for an individual to squeeze into the British team. That is changing now but because there are still so few people taking part, it remains true of some sports.'

Ian Thompson describes the problem this way: 'In sports and categories which attract the smallest numbers of competitors, the national level and grassroots level are virtually the same. The problem however is that if the categories and classifications are too broad, then a number of competitors with severe disabilities could be pushed out of the Paralympics.'

'That is one of the things we've got to guard against,' says Tanni, 'but I still think that sports where there are only four or five people competing shouldn't be included.'

By June 1994, there was no better way to demonstrate Tanni's domination of the wheelchair-racing field than by referring to the programme of the British Wheelchair Sports Foundation's second National Wheelchair Championship, held at Stoke Mandeville.

All the current national records were laid out. Tanni was shown to be seven minutes slower in the marathon than her nearest rival Rose Hill. Yet when it came to the other track distances, the name of Tanni Grey was untouchable. The British records set during various times in 1992 and 1993 for 100, 200, 400, 800, 1500, 5,000 and 10,000 metres, were all held by Tanni. And this was making no allowances for the fact that she is a T3, and not a T4. Tanni also still dominated the road-racing with a 10km record established in the United States the year before and the half-marathon record established in Portsmouth.

The only other athlete to sweep the board in quite the same way was Peter Carruthers, unbeatable in the open quadriplegic class, with British records in all seven track and five road-racing events.

More was to come for in July, in Berlin, Tanni broke the world record 400 metres again in a new time of 58.38 seconds. If at one time it might have been feared that she had reached her best at the Barcelona Paralympics, there was now no doubt that she was capable of extending herself and breaking further times.

Ian certainly believes that Tanni can achieve even better times for almost all events. What she needs is sharper competition to bring out the best in her. At present, she has to travel the world to race against people who are at her level of attainment.

Berlin was the venue for the World Championships, where Tanni not only won the 400 metres but the Gold in the 100 metres as well. In the 1500 and 5,000 metres final, she also set new British records. Her 100-metre time was 17.93 seconds and in the 800 metres it was 2 minutes 0.23 seconds, scoring another Gold. The 1500 metres was rather more disappointing and Tanni only managed sixth place in 3 minutes 42.89 seconds and in the 5,000 metres, although she set a new British record of 13 minutes 09.54

seconds, she also managed to get a sixth place. Her third Gold of the Games came when she won the 200 metres in 30.75 seconds.

Tanni's experience as a T3 sprinter was showing. She came away from the Games with four Golds and a Bronze plus two new world records. After a brief stopover at her home in Heath, she was off again, this time heading for Helsinki to compete in an 800-metres exhibition race during the European Athletics Championships. She won a Bronze with a time of 2 minutes 08.28 seconds.

These achievements at the World Championships rivalled those of Barcelona. Her total haul, the Gold in 100, 200, 400 and 800 metres and the Bronze in the 10,000 metres, plus world records in the 200 and 400 metres and British records in the 1500, 5,000 and 10,000 metres distances, were very satisfying. Having concentrated in particular on the 200 and 400 metres, the fact that she achieved new world-record times pleased her greatly.

'The standard of competition has really improved,' she observed afterwards, 'so it was nice to show that I could still hold my own. We were competing in the old Olympic stadium – a pretty impressive venue.'

Tanni was accompanied on that occasion by her father and Sian who were there to celebrate Tanni's twenty-fifth birthday. They however felt that the atmosphere in Berlin had none of the spark of Barcelona.

'It was a let-down,' Sian said. 'Sometimes Dad and I were the only people in the stadium who had paid to watch. The competition was very good but, thanks to a lack of publicity, there were very few spectators and little atmosphere.'

From Tanni's point of view, there were none of the comforts and welcoming touches of Barcelona. The heat was stifling, the place she was given to stay in was an hour's bus ride away from the stadium and getting from the warm-up track to the stadium posed unforeseen problems.

'The buses weren't air-conditioned,' Tanni recalls, 'and, in particular with the severe heat, a number of athletes became

191

dehydrated.' Tanni herself had to ensure that she was drinking at least ten litres of fluid every day.

Between 18–28 August 1994, British Columbia in Canada hosted the fifteenth Commonwealth Games in Victoria. An exhibition event was arranged for disability sport but there was no event in which Tanni could appear. The English men's wheelchair team was however looking for a manager/ administrator and, because Tanni had experience chairing the BWRA, it was an obvious move to ask her to do the job. This involved Tanni in being teased and ragged by the Welsh men's wheelchair team because, normally fiercely proud of her Welsh ancestry, she was required to wear an English kit.

The appearance of wheelchair athletes at the Games might have passed off as a minor event almost unnoticed by the international media and largely forgotten by the spectators, had it not been for the outspoken remarks of an Australian official, Norman Tunstall. His petulant display of prejudice against the presence of disabled athletes at the games created a great deal of publicity which completely backfired on him.

'We have quite a lot to thank him for,' says Tanni. 'And, in a sense, I admire the guy because he had the guts to say what many people were thinking but wouldn't say. Of course I don't agree with him but he's entitled to his opinion.

'My perception, from years of being in wheelchair sport, is that a lot of people don't come into contact with disabilities, don't understand about sport, and don't understand what is involved for people who dedicate their lives to disability sport.

'As far as dedication is concerned, there's actually very little difference between disabled and able-bodied athletes. Both train as much and both sacrifice a great deal of their lives to sporting excellence. While many people, through ignorance, do not know this, I would rather people be honest and say "I don't think you're a proper athlete" than to cover it up with over-polite coyness.'

Yet it was not her status as an athlete that came into question when Tanni went to Victoria, it was her acceptability as an official.

This made her especially angry and even more aware of the distance that disabled people still had to travel to improve attitudes. When the organizers of the Commonwealth Games realized that the person attached to the English men's wheelchair team would also be in a wheelchair, they felt that this would not be appropriate. This was partly because, in the past, it had been the pattern that athletes with disabilities had been accompanied by able-bodied officials or team managers.

Tanni had a call from Norman Sarsfield, the English team manager. The gist of his message was that, as she was a woman and a wheelchair-user, it might be better if she did not come as an official.

Tanni was astounded. She realized that many people had that kind of attitude, but for someone to say it to her outright was a dreadful cheek and not something she was going to accept.

It might be easier sometimes, Tanni acknowledges, if there were able-bodied people to assist Paralympic athletes to carry their heavy things around. But when it comes to anything to do with the politics of disability or the sport itself, then she feels that there is absolutely no reason why a disabled person should not be there.

Tanni's value as a team official was that she knew the rules of wheelchair-racing and had experience of competing at major events herself. If she, as part of her job, needed to lodge an official complaint she would therefore have the knowledge to quote the grounds and rules.

It was also suggested that as she was a woman there might be other problems with accommodation. But that was not a problem for Tanni.

'When we compete in Switzerland or most European events,' she says, 'all the accommodation and all the showers are communal.'

Tanni was told Mr Sarsfield's call was not meant to be patronizing but some officials felt that she might not be able to do the job. At the British Paralympic Association some felt that Tanni should not make too big a fuss about the issue.

In the end, the officials backed down and Tanni had her own room in the block of flats which she shared with the male athletes.

'I don't know whether being with all those men was supposed to be a punishment, but it certainly wasn't a hardship watching all those gorgeous legs of the English boxers, swimmers and cyclists walk past me every morning!'

After the Games, it should be noted that Norman Sarsfield was forthright in his praise for Tanni. 'All my collegues and I had grave doubts about whether she could cope. But we were wrong, everything worked absolutely perfectly.'

There were also, Tanni feels, a few people in the able-bodied team who found it hard to cope with an official in a wheelchair. Tanni could not fail to notice the stand-offish attitudes. But one event changed things amazingly.

She went to the English office to check the mail box for information about the day's events and at that moment Linford Christie, the star of the Games, arrived. Tanni recalls everyone swarming around him and treating him as the VIP he was and still is. Amid all this, Tanni went into the office and two people said, in a rather off-hand manner, 'I suppose you want the mail'. At that moment Linford Christie turned round and, seeing Tanni, took her by the hand, gave her a great big hug and kiss, and said 'Miss Grey! How are you?'.

Tanni, determined to be cool in the circumstances, greeted him with, 'Hi Linford! How are you doing?'.

Following this incident, any negative attitudes towards her changed for the better. Linford and Tanni had met in the course of the BBC *Children in Need* appeal as well as on various other occasions and he had followed her career.

'After that,' Tanni remembers, 'acceptance built up as people began to understand. Most of the initial reaction was just lack of understanding.'

During the Games, Tanni noticed other changes in attitudes. The cycling team for instance were quick to spot that they had much in common with the wheelchair athletes. They began by questioning the Paralympic athletes about their equipment, especially the carbon-fibre wheels and then, because the similarities between the two sports were so great, began comparing other pieces of equipment.

Tanni also found herself helping out with the boxers. The Games are known as the 'friendly Games' and Tanni was able to help one of the young competitors struggling to sew a strap by taking the needle and cotton from him and finishing the job.

'In due course the ice really broke between the Paralympic and able-bodied athletes. The atmosphere was great. It was good to be with them, actually living together, because they could see what our training involved.'

As a team official, Tanni only had four English track athletes in her squad – Ian Thompson, David Holding, Jack McKenna and Ivan Newman. Unfamiliar with the rules of swimming at an international level, she felt that she would not be a great deal of use and was not involved with this.

Halfway through the Games, Tanni had further contact, at a reception, with the officials who had tried to keep her away. While some were very pleasant, others were, Tanni recalls, 'patronizing'. One actually introduced her to others as his 'little friend'. Then at the end of the evening, the officials began singing a military marching song and decided that, instead of doing all the usual marching actions, they would pretend to push a wheelchair instead. Tanni found this particularly infuriating because it was supposedly being done to make her feel at home. She left as soon as she could and returned to the athletes village.

'It was really very offensive. They were standing in a big circle, singing this song and pretending, with arm actions, to push a wheelchair.'

Back in the village, she found some of the lads from the team. She had not made a fuss at the reception, leaving at the earliest opportunity, but when the team began asking: 'Did you have a nice time, swanning off to the reception?', Tanni expressed her annoyance. Tanni has no reason to believe that the officials from the English team meant in any way to be deliberately offensive.

'It showed,' she said, 'just a complete lack of understanding about people with disabilities. It was very similar in feeling to them saying that I couldn't go as a team manager.'

Looking back, she does feel that attitudes to disability sport changed at the Games and that this was thanks to the presence and influence of the men's squad.

In England again, Tanni's family tried unsuccessfully to tell her to slow down for the 1995 season. There was no need, they said, for her to accept every invitation to every race. But Tanni is 'addicted' to her sport and any opportunity to race is eagerly taken up. Of one of the well-established events in the sporting calendar, she will say: 'This year I won't be doing that particular race', but then before her family knows it, she is in the car with her racing chair and off to take part.

However, the 1995 season did not see Tanni lining up in Blackheath for the London Marathon. Instead, by way of a change and a new challenge, she chose to take part in the 99th Boston Marathon and watch the London from the sidelines – or at least a BBC commentary position.

Accompanied to Boston by Sian, who was taking a holiday from her staff nurse post at the University Hospital of Wales, the two of them took the opportunity to see the sights. A postcard, showing an illustrated map of New England, was sent addressed to Mr and Mrs P A H Grey and Chum, the dog, with the news: 'Been there, seen it, done it, bought the T-shirt'.

The Boston event attracts almost all the top international names. So from Tanni's point of view this was an even greater challenge than the London Marathons, where the international competitors have been absent.

The best time had been recorded by Jean Driscoll from Illinois who, in 1994, finished in 1 hour 34 minutes 22 seconds. Over four years the winning time had come down by over nine minutes. The wheelchair-racers set off at 11.45 am on Monday 17 April through the American east coast city and Tanni, wearing Number C107, finished sixth. Jean Driscoll again won the event but in a significantly slower time of 1 hour 47 minutes 43 seconds.

Rose Hill, Tanni's main marathon rival, chose to take part in both events, even though there were only two weeks between them. She was the only female wheelchair athlete to take part in the London Marathon and finished behind Tanni in Boston. Rose appreciates that her weakness in the marathon, her specialist event, is that she does not have the kick at the end to sprint to the finish.

'Hilly and I didn't have a very good race in Boston,' Tanni admits. 'It wasn't a good time. I had just had a new race chair and there was a bit of a problem with a wheel, which I had to stop to fix.'

Rose hopes that she will soon be able to beat Tanni at the longer distances and is now working with a new Canadian coach. She has been training to take part in some of the shorter track events to give her more experience of sprint finishes and a degree of extra speed. She found that this work paid off at the Berlin Marathon in 1995 where she came second, finishing ahead of Tanni. In past marathons, she has had to lose Tanni very quickly because if Tanni stays with her it is Tanni who can overhaul her at the line. Rose is determined to put an end to this. Her aim is to set the world record for the women's wheelchair marathon.

Tanni versus Rose in a marathon might not be quite as aggressive as Hill versus Schumacher on the motor-racing circuit, but there is still a sharp, competitive edge to each event.

'We race side by side,' says Tanni, 'not working together. We also race for different companies, so there is additional rivalry through this.'

Unless, that is, one or other of them has managed to grab a good lead at an early stage.

Less than two weeks after Tanni and Sian had crossed the Atlantic from Boston, Tanni was competing in very different surroundings keeping up her commitment to the sport at grass roots in Britain. She was in Sheffield to take part in the wheelchair half-marathon and won her event in 57 minutes 26 seconds.

Tanni has always been willing to lend her name and reputation to launch products which might advance the mobility of wheelchair-users. The interest in Tanni's endorsement results from the provision of chairs and chair aids for disabled people becoming an increasingly competitive market. At the regular trade exhibitions, the manufacturers compete with their latest products, many of which have been updated for home use on the back of improvements developed for racing chairs.

One example of this came in May when, in the course of opening a new cycle trail through Afan Argoed Forest Park near Port Talbot, Tanni tried out a special tandem bicycle which would enable disabled visitors to take to the park trails. The tandem, which had both steering and hand pedals at the front, together with a standard bicycle at the back, had been developed by a firm in East Sussex at the cost of £3,800. It had a twenty-one speed mountain bike gear system and the wheelchair part could be used either attached to the front of the bicycle, with the person behind doing the pedalling, or could be powered jointly with the crank mechanism in the front. This would enable the wheelchair-user to propel the machine with his or her arms.

Tanni explains that she has many requests to sponsor products but has to keep a hard business head when deciding which to endorse: 'I was once asked to do promotions for a tyre company but all they were offering me was a free set of tyres!'

By the spring of 1995, the British Paralympic Association was publishing the latest diary of events for Atlanta. It was still provisional and the spring 1995 version was revised from a previous calendar. Tanni, along with many other potential Paralympians, was becoming increasingly concerned about the way the Games would turn out. There was still so much uncertainty about when events would take place and who would be entitled to take part.

Six months later, much of the Atlanta programme was still up for grabs and some Paralympians were anxiously remembering that the last time the Americans had been the Olympic hosts, the Paralympic Games had fallen by the wayside. In October of that year *The Economist* magazine felt that the issues were important enough to run a perceptive piece looking at the Paralympic dilemma. To introduce the general reader to the sports, they accompanied the article with a picture of Tanni in action and the piece began with a flashback:

Barcelona, 1992. A British racer, Tanni Grey, and her Danish rival, Ingrid Lauridson, were battling for first place in the women's 100 metre sprint. Ninety metres into the race, Miss Lauridson was ahead by a nose, and for an instant it looked as if Miss Grey, the record-holding world champion, was about to be ousted. It was one of the most dramatic races of the summer – yet few television viewers could watch it; hardly any newspapers reported it; no Olympic medals were handed out for it. Why the neglect? Miss Grey and Miss Lauridson were racing in wheelchairs. They were competing in 'parallel' games for people with disabilities.

Though two wheelchair races were held as exhibition events at the Olympic Games in Los Angeles, Seoul and Barcelona – and will again take place at Atlanta – no disabled sport has ever been a full-medal event at the Olympics. Officials grumble that the Olympics can only expand so much. But over the past three Olympic cycles, they have made room for lots of new events, including table tennis, badminton and baseball. At next year's summer games, team rhythmic gymnastics and mountain biking will join the official roster. Ballroom dancing and kite flying will be on display.

Meanwhile, the world's finest wheelchairs racers, blind swimmers and seated volleyball players compete in a separate competition, the Paralympics (known as the 'crip Olympics' by disabled athletes). The Paralympics and the Olympics have much in common. Both are elitist, permitting only the best to compete. Since 1988, they have been using the same stadiums, pools and tracks. (The Paralympics take place in the ten or so days following the main games.) And both have kept expanding. New Paralympic events continue to be added, and the number of athletes swells: some 4,000 disabled competitors will tussle next year in Atlanta, compared with only 400 in Rome in 1960.

The article explained how broadcasters were reluctant to televise the events, feeling there was not enough demand from the viewers. The International Olympic Committee have also seemed content to keep themselves separate from the Paralympics, complaining about its counterpart's logo which, they said, resembled the Olympic rings too closely.

The feature argued that the message that this ongoing separation conveyed was that disabled athletes, however excellent, were still different. Rick Hansen, a leader in the fight for integration was quoted as saying 'There's an important transition to make from thinking of disabled athletes, to thinking of athletes who just happen to have disabilities.'

Hansen is chairman of CIAD (the Committee for the Integration of Athletes with a Disability), set up by the IPC to look at adding disabled sport to the Olympics. CIAD has proposed that women's 800 metre and men's 1,500 metre wheelchair racing be raised to full-medal status at the Olympics by 2000. The feature continued:

> Not everybody is pleased. Ironically, the plan's fiercest opponents come from within the disabled movement itself. The British Paralympic Association, for example, supports demonstration sports at the Olympics, to raise awareness, but thinks full-medal status will be disastrous. The Olympics will pinch two or three of their best sports and finest athletes, says Barry Schofield, the Association's general secretary, then leave the rest of the Paralympic games to crumble.
>
> Indeed, integration is not as simple as it appears. After wheelchair racing, what other Paralympic sports should be included – and on what grounds? Sitting volleyball might make the excitement grade, but what will happen to cerebral-palsy boccia – or to 'goalball', a sport where the audience has to keep silent so that sightless players can hear the movements of the ball? Realistically speaking, no more than a handful of disabled sports could even hope to make full Olympic status, even if they met tight IOC criteria for inclusion.

Another issue is whether 'walkies' or 'able bods' should be allowed to compete in disabled sports. In goalball, for instance, players with different degrees of sight play together, but they are blindfolded to ensure an equal handicap. Why could a sighted person not play?

Nobody within the IPC doubts the value of adding disabled events to able-bodied sport – but there is a feud about exactly how it should be done. Many feel the better strategy is to aim for lesser competitions, such as the Commonwealth Games and the European Championships. (Both now host demonstration events.) These events, they feel, will not compromise the Paralympics Games as the Olympics might.

All this background uncertainty concerning the future of the sport has not however held back the further advancement of disability sport as far as the media is concerned. The news and sports channel, BBC Radio 5 Live, started a run of fifteen-minute specials called *Sport First* to focus on all aspects of sport for people with disabilities.

Donna Howarth produced the programme, which was a live input into Radio 5's evening schedule, from Manchester. Tanni was asked to present it and for three months she travelled every Tuesday to work on the scripts and record material prior to broadcast.

In broadcasting, as with racing, Tanni's nerves were tested to the extreme. But as her sister Sian puts it, 'It's only if Tanni doesn't worry and feel sick that you have to concerned. That's when she doesn't put in her best performance'.

'There were a few occasions when I thought I needed a bucket in the studio,' Tanni says, 'but I coped.'

In between her regular engagements, there were international and national events. Tanni took part in most of the competitions she had attended regularly over the years, marathons, half-marathons and other track events. The list of places she has visited reads like the departure board at an airport: Sweden, Australia, Florida, USA, Germany, France, Canada, to name a few – many of them visited two or three times.

201

There were other engagements too, the sort that any celebrity fits into the diary. In June, Tanni was involved in the official opening of extended facilities at Marks and Spencer in Swansea.

In the same month, at the invitation of the High Sheriff of Mid-Glamorgan, she had lunch at the Law Courts in Cardiff. Then, as well as being on the Lottery Sports Panel, the committee helping to distribute some of the lottery money to sport, she helped judge a young people's design competition.

For Sulwen however the gold embossed card from the Lord Chamberlain, 'commanded by Her Majesty to invite' Tanni and her mother to a garden party at Buckingham Palace on 13 July was the highlight. The palace garden party was milling with the throngs of people who attend, drawn from the great, the good, the worthy and the unsung from all over the kingdom.

'How do people get to meet the Queen?' someone wondered aloud as they waited. 'It's probably already arranged in advance' it was decided.

However, as Sulwen and Tanni were waiting with the crowds, they were approached by an official who, having spoken briefly to them, asked if they would like to meet the monarch.

It was a moment which Sulwen has tucked in her memory for ever. She and Tanni spoke to the Queen at some length, with the Queen asking about training and competing. Then she asked Sulwen whether she watched her daughter race and Sulwen explained that she was too frightened to do so. 'Quite understandable' Her Majesty replied. The Queen was also concerned about how Tanni managed to push her chair across the grass and heard how a new shale gravel path in the palace gardens had caused problems. Then, wishing them well and hoping they enjoyed the tea, the Queen moved on.

One of the topics the Queen introduced into the conversation was Tanni's next major event abroad – the World Athletics Championships in Gothenburg. They discussed what the weather was likely to be and Tanni was wished well.

Tanni had secured her qualifying time for Gothenburg for the 800 metres of 2 minutes 12.09 seconds when racing in the

Toronto Wheelchair Challenge. She had also won the 100, 200 and the 400 metres, in the T3 class, showing that she was still the world leader. The Gothenburg Exhibition Race however was open category so Tanni would be up against the world's top T4s as well.

At 3 o'clock on 12 August, wearing Number 473, she came within 0.75 seconds of winning the event. She was in fact fourth behind Louise Sauvage from Australia, Chantal Peticlerc from Canada and DeAnna Sodama from America. There was no room for any disappointment and no other T3 racer could have got anywhere closer.

Indeed in the T3 category, the only possible challenge in Atlanta is likely to come from Francesca Porcellato from Italy. Tracey Lewis however has her mind firmly set on the Games and, after her break from sport, is she believes showing good form. Yet even if she is selected, she will know she has never beaten Tanni on the track and Tanni has the age advantage.

It is noticeable that in wheelchair racing, even on the track, age is not the factor it might be in some sports. Certainly Linford Christie has stayed on top of the world in his thirties and Rose Hill, some fifteen years older than Tanni, has now taken up track events in earnest. In Atlanta however Rose will not be a threat because she is in a different classification from Tanni.

Whether any other British women emerge with potential as athletes will largely depend on whether they can show dedication to training and get access to the right equipment. There are some charities which help provide racing chairs but the resources are limited and the machines are becoming more expensive each year. £2,000 to buy the best. In other countries, especially the USA and Australia, the situation is different and it could be that Tanni's real competition on the Atlanta track will emerge from these two countries.

Not taking anything for granted, Tanni with her coaches has planned a training programme to see her through the 1995/96 autumn and winter season. She knows Atlanta will have special problems, notably the heat. This will be particularly sapping during the long events. She will need to decide whether to restrict herself in distance or go for events across the board.

For the Games themselves to be a triumph and for her to achieve success, Tanni knows that other things apart from her fitness and form are important.

What compromise will eventually be reached, she wonders, between the Games's organizers and those championing the cause of athletes with learning disabilities? Will sufficient money be raised from sponsors and other sources to put on the same sort of Games as seen in Barcelona? Also, will the Games be free from tragedy and scandal? Might the sapping heat prove too much for some of the competitors? Will cheating and drug-taking mar the spirit of the Games? Will the public in America be as enthusiastic as the Barcelonians? Will the Games, in general, live up to the expectations that so many people around the world now have of the Paralympics?

One thing is certain, the elite Paralympians will without a doubt put on a sporting spectacle as exciting as any that their able-bodied colleagues can produce.

CHAPTER EIGHT

Future plans

*'There are times when we wish Tanni would slow down
and not pack so much into her days.'*
Sulwen Grey

A FEW DAYS AFTER the World Championships in Berlin in 1993 the phone rang at Tanni's home in Heath. Sulwen answered. It was one of the senior sports officials: Could Tanni phone him when she returned? It did not matter what time of day or night, she had to ring. There was no indication as to what this was about, but Sulwen detected that it was a serious matter.

Tanni had hoped to be back in good time that day but, as it happened, her car did not pull up outside her home until eight o'clock in the evening.

By that time Sulwen's imagination had been working overtime. Not only was she wondering about the important message, she was also worrying about Tanni. Unusually, Tanni had not put through a quick phone call home to say that she would be late and Sulwen was both anxious and angry that she had not heard a word.

She immediately gave Tanni the message. Tanni went to the phone and a few minutes later came in to the room.

'Daniela's dead,' she said and began to cry.

'It was horrible,' Tanni says. 'It took a long long time to sink in and I just couldn't believe that she wouldn't be around any more.'

Sulwen then tried to coax more information out of Tanni and it transpired that Daniela Jutzeler, a good friend and fellow sportswoman, had been killed in a road-traffic accident a short while before.

The Swiss wheelchair racer had been training for the European Games when she had been hit by a lorry and died instantly.

Tanni had known Daniela as a fellow competitor for six years, having met her first in Dallas in 1988. She was a couple of years older than Tanni but they had much in common, especially training routines, which in both their cases included considerable mileage on roads. Tanni and Daniela had been good friends and Daniela had helped and encouraged Tanni in her career.

The main difference between the two was that while Tanni had been disabled through spina bifida, Daniela had become a wheelchair user following a firearms accident.

'It was a twist of fate,' Tanni said, 'that the family found very difficult to deal with. Daniela was a really attractive girl and it took her a long time to accept her new life. It was only during the last year that everything had really come together for her. She had begun to do a lot of television reporting, had settled down with her boyfriend, was about to buy a home and had become a national heroine in Switzerland. She had everything and yet it didn't save her.

'One of the worst things was that, almost immediately afterwards, I had to fly to Helsinki for the European Games. Daniela's death affected everyone. All the athletes wore black arm-bands and there was a minute's silence before the race. I just sat there on the starting line trying not to cry. Everyone was the same. It was really hard.

'It was also rather confusing because we were meant to have a minute's silence just before the medal presentation, but instead had it before the start. That disturbed a lot of athletes who were also very confused because the silence was announced to spectators in four languages.

'Having been at the starting line, feeling very emotional, I then had to get my head around the race and be ready for that.

As it was, I didn't race well. Not only was I upset by the news of Daniela's death, but I was more tired than I expected after the World Championships. Perhaps it would have been better to have cancelled the race, but all the athletes had considered that possibility and we all decided that we should do the race for Daniela. That is what she would have wanted.'

The race was an exhibition event, as part of the able-bodied Games. Few in the crowd or the commentary boxes quite realized what was going on when all the wheelchair athletes appeared wearing mourning. The circuit of elite athletes is, despite rivalries, a close-knit one and everyone was deeply affected. Daniela had been a very popular figure, right at the forefront of the development of the sport.

Daniela's accident also made Tanni and the other athletes realize that all sports pushed to their limits have dangers.

For a number of years, following the death of someone at Loughborough in 1989 who was not wearing head protection, Tanni had worn a crash helmet when training on the streets. She continued to wear it even though people wondered why and questioned whether it was necessary.

It is now compulsory to wear head protection when racing. On track, wheelchair racing is not a soft option and this fact was reinforced in the Barcelona Paralympic Games when there was a spectacular multiple pile-up in the men's 5,000 metres. Fortunately there were no major injuries, but competitors and chairs were strewn across the track.

On roads, the chairs regularly reach speeds of over 20 mph and go even faster downhill with wind assistance. Tanni is well aware that she needs to wear conspicuous clothing when on the roads and always ensures, when training at night, that her chair is well lit. However well known she is in the neighbourhood of Heath, there is always the possibility of motorists who are not familiar with the sight of Tanni out training, and she is always conscious of the risks of an accident.

Peter and Sulwen are also both very aware of the dangers, and are relieved that Tanni wears bright clothes when out on the road. She now avoids training at dusk, when the light is particularly bad, and after Daniela's accident put a warning flag on her chair.

When someone in their mid-twenties loses a friend and colleague so tragically and abruptly, some of life's deeper questions come into sharper focus. Although almost every hour of Tanni's waking life is devoted in one way or another to her career, she realizes that this will not always be the case. There is only a certain period of one's life in which one can afford to be totally single-minded and dedicated, otherwise one becomes a narrow, self-focused individual. Life is about relationships, fulfilment in a wide sphere of activities and about knowing oneself.

There is however a certain fatalism in Tanni's views on life. She accepts and does not begrudge her disability.

'Because of it and because of what I have made of it, I realize that my life has offered me greater opportunities. No one can change what cannot be changed but, if you are in the right place at the right time, much can be achieved.'

Hers is truly a fatalistic philosophy on life.

Does this mean, therefore, that Tanni sees life as a form of uncontrollable chaos, or is there some form of guidance at work?

For someone who has thought deeply about many issues, Tanni shies away from questions such as these. She sits very much on a philosophical fence, saying that she is neither religious nor an atheist. She is not sure whether there is a God, but she believes there is something beyond the material.

In her childhood she attended church, and indeed won her certificate for Bible knowledge, but now she does not particularly enjoy acts of worship. She comes from a Welsh Methodist background on her mother's side and an Anglican background on her father's. Sulwen was confirmed an Anglican as an adult in 1995, and Tanni was glad that she was there in the church to see her mother go forward and declare her faith. She talks of this as a moving moment.

'Mum has always found a lot of support from the church and for her it was just a question of finding the right church. For me it was good to be there at the service because Mum has given me so much support and it was nice to give her some support in return.'

Peter and Tanni have great debates. Her father acknowledges that they probably have opposite views on the majority of subjects, but maybe that is because Tanni has a lot of confidence. Tanni and Sian, also gang up together to rag him affectionately. Peter has a particular dislike of the small magnet ornaments that can be attached to kitchen refrigerators, so Tanni and Sian have now bought him so many that they now use them to spell messages to each other on the fridge door!

The relationship between parents and children evolves over the years from one of total dependence to the eventual loosening of ties and the option of being good friends or just acquaintances. Tanni spends much of her time away travelling but the family home she has known since her first days is still her base. That is where people telephone her, and where Sulwen takes the messages and checks the diary. That is where she keeps her books and papers, spare parts, clothing and so on. Sian too is based at home, leaving at various times of day or night depending on her work pattern at the University Hospital of Wales where she is a staff nurse in the high-dependency unit.

Their father is now retired from his job with the Health Service and therefore has the time to be much more involved with Tanni's career. He is a careful, methodical man and a talented artist. Indeed, Tanni describes both her father and Ian Thompson as the sensible ones who keep her in line. Tanni and Ian, having started out with a common interest in wheelchair sport, have become much closer and Tanni spends what time she can with him at his home in Redcar.

'My dad is amazingly sensible and perhaps I don't give him enough credit to his face for that. I tend to wind him up a bit. When he's being really serious with me I bring out "Woogi", my fluffy, yellow finger puppet and have conversations with it. So, for instance, when Dad tries to talk about pensions and planning, I have conversations with Woogi.

'My approach must annoy him endlessly, but I respect a lot of what he says to me, although it probably doesn't seem to him that I take it all that seriously. He's very good at keeping me in line and Ian's the same, though he probably has a more effective way of telling me what I should do. He takes a more psychological approach in giving me advice and avoids confrontations.'

Tanni and her father have a very different approach to organization.

'Tanni is happy to get on a plane and go without any accommodation being arranged in advance. I would only be comfortable getting on the plane knowing that I had a hotel booking,' he says.

It is Sulwen who takes a lot of responsibility for the administration of Tanni's disparate and whirlwind career. Tanni admits that she tends to dump a lot of things on her mother who is very patient with her. Between Sulwen, her father and Ian, she is kept organized.

As well as managing her own affairs, Tanni has been very involved with the British Wheelchair Racing Association committee and, when she is away competing, a lot of paperwork to do with the Association arrives. Tanni finds she dumps it onto other people, with Ian often picking up the pieces.

Through the BWRA, Tanni is caught up in the politics of her sport and indirectly involved in organizing training weekends for beginners and others interested in the sport. She is also involved in the arrangements for the road racing Grand Prix, and helps to negotiate prize money and sponsorship.

On top of all her other commitments in 1995, Tanni continued, as often as time permitted with her post-graduate research. She found it harder than she had expected because there was so little historical information available on disability sport.

She is nevertheless keen to pursue the work during her hectic timetable so that she can take a more informed view of what changes need to take place and have a fuller understanding of the problems.

'I would like to do more historical research with people who were around when the movement started,' she says.

BBC Radio 5 Live's approach to Tanni and her subsequent presenting of the series of fifteen minute evening programmes on disability sport, has given her another pointer as to what she might do in the future. In many ways the broadcasts were not a cost effective use of her time, but they might prove to be an important part of Tanni's long-term strategy. Her personality and on-air presentation make her a natural broadcaster. There are only a few sportsmen and women who have successfully made the transition from competitor to commentator. Most who have excelled in one field have not been able to adapt to the next. All the signs are that Tanni will be able to do so, spreading her expertise to cover not only disability sport but other sports as well. A future for her could well lie in the media.

Additionally, if she completes her Master's thesis, academic options could open to her as well. Her keenness to become involved in the long-term planning of her sport could also mean that she may have an important part to play there. Inevitably, her particular emphasis would be on setting up the structure to allow children with disabilities at school to have better physical education and wider options to choose sports at which some of them will in due course excel.

Although she is so closely involved with her sport, Tanni does sometimes look ahead and think that she would like to do something that had absolutely nothing to do with disability.

'At one level or another, my whole life is wheelchair racing, and there are times when I get fed up with it and think I would like to do something else. I discuss this with Ian who races because he loves it, but has to work for a living. My whole life however is wheelchair racing. I train, I work, I do voluntary work all for the sport. I'm involved at different committee levels with disability sport; my Masters degree is on disability sport; if I ever go and do anything, it's about disability sport. It all gets a bit much sometimes. There is a lot of pressure, all of my own making.

211

'So therefore I do dream about being away from it. Though I don't think I ever will be because I care a lot about it and the way it's going and the way it's organized and I think athletes should have a much bigger input in what they're doing. A lot of athletes are not interested and that's their choice. A lot of athletes don't know how to become involved in the decision-making processes. But the movement is young and I think it's important for everybody to work together more closely rather than fighting each other within the system.'

The internal conflicts within the disability movement certainly need to be tackled, though exactly how this will be done Tanni is still not clear. In some ways through her work with the BWRA representing other wheelchair athletes, she is involved in yet another fragmentation of the movement.

That Tanni will be influential in years to come in the field of disability politics is undoubted. In January 1996 she was appointed as one of the 17 members of the new National Disability Council set up under the Disability Discrimination Act to advise the Secretary of State on matters relating to disability and monitor the working of the new legislation. She was one of the majority on the council with direct experience of disability and joined a banker, business people and a trade union leader.

On a personal level, Ian – like Peter – is concerned that Tanni takes on too much in an unstructured manner. He admits to being a 'bit of a drifter' himself and is perhaps well placed to see that tendency in someone else. He feels that perhaps she needs a manager or agent, someone who can help organize her career and help her select the best options. He also feels she needs to ask some tough questions about her research: Is this what she really wants to do at the moment and can she do it justice fitting it in and around so many other attractions and possibilities? 'She gets pulled in all directions and needs professional advice on setting goals and priorities.'

One day, Tanni's track career will inevitably come to an end. Because hers is such a young sport no one knows how long an elite competitor can stay at the top before age and injuries take their toll. Peter says that he would advise his daughter to give up if she was unsure of turning out stylish performances.

'That does not mean that she always has to win, but she has to race well. I think she could go on well into her thirties if she wanted to. But would she be happy? There will come a time when even Tanni will be turning up and thinking that there's something else she would rather be doing. I would be prepared to advise her to give up if necessary, but by then I would probably be a year too late. Tanni has got to a stage in her chosen profession where nobody can predict the peak or the plateau and therefore I think she will go over the top before she actually gives up.'

Tanni takes a pragmatic approach and realizes that every year it gets harder to train – especially throughout the winter. She acknowledges that there is bound to be a time when things other than racing will be of more interest to her.

'I do not know what these things might be. I would like to develop my work in radio and perhaps public relations. I would also be quite interested in having a proper nine-to-five job for a while, to see what that would be like. But at present, I'm working towards Atlanta and I'm keeping all my options open for afterwards.'

Peter and Sulwen continue to look on their younger daughter's career as an athlete with an amazement. Little could they have realized when they first met that they would, in due course, become the pivot around which the successful career of an athlete and sports personality would prosper. Certainly at the time of Tanni's birth, in those first days when the news was broken to them that their child had a disability, they could not have dreamt of Tanni becoming an athlete.

'There are times,' Sulwen admits, 'when we wish that Tanni would slow down and not pack so much into her days. But, on the other hand, what would we be thinking if she had turned out differently? If she'd been one of those people who are content to sit in a chair all day not wanting to do anything?

'Obviously we're immensely proud of her for what she's

achieved, and especially for the way that she presents a positive image of a person with a disability and of disabled sport. One day people will begin to pay more attention to the abilities and potential of disabled people rather than the disability. Tanni is doing the pioneering work.

I think we have been fortunate to have had a determined child like Tanni. She has brought a lot of joy.'

List of key races

1986 National Games
Stoke Mandeville
100m   22.8
200m   47.9

1987 National Games
Stoke Mandeville
100m   22.9
200m   46.8
400m   1.39.7

1987 International Games
Stoke Mandeville
100m   22.16
200m   44.29

1987 Vienna Games
100m   22.43 (1st)
200m   45.37 (2nd)
400m   1.43.0 (3rd)

1988 National Disabled Student Games
Loughborough
60m   14.0
100m   22.0
Slalom   1.43.0

1988 National Wheelchair Games
Stoke Mandeville
100m   21.8
400m   1.31.0

1988 Nautilus Classic
Dallas
100m   21.15 (3rd)
200m   41.69 (3rd)
400m   1.22.01 (5th)

1988 Queen of the Straight
Stoke Mandeville
100m   20.8

1988 Paralympics
Seoul
100m   20.64
200m   42.05
400m   1.22.72 (Bronze)

1989 Irish National Games
100m   20.6
200m   43.6
400m   1.25.1

1989 Swiss Nationals
100m   21.19
200m   40.31
400m   1.21.75
800m   2.45.69

1989 BWRA National Track Championships
Mansfield
100m   21.6
200m   40.6
400m   1.21.3
800m   2.52.5
1500m   5.32.4
(won all events)

British Wheelchair Marathon
Porthcawl
              3.00.4.0

1990 Commonwealth Games
Auckland
800m   2.27

215

1990 BWRA National Track Championships
Birmingham
100m   22.2
200m   40.7
400m   1.16.4
800m   2.47.4
1500m   5.21.2
5000m   18.29.1
(won all events)

1990 London Marathon
2.49.54.0 (4th)

1990 National Wheelchair Games
Stoke Mandeville
100m   20.8 (1st)
200m   36.4 (1st)
400m   1.15.0 (1st)
800m   2.34.2 (1st)
1500m   4.46.7

1990 World Championships
Holland
100m   20.38 (2nd)
200m   36.41 (2nd)
400m   1.12.11 (3rd)
800m   2.38.54 (4th)
Marathon 2.20.25.0 (1st)

1990 World Wheelchair Games
Stoke Mandeville
100m   21.1
200m   36.85
400m   1.10.86

1990 Queen of the Straight
Stoke Mandeville
100m   19.14

1990 Cardiff Games Invitation
1500m   4.48.13 (1st)

1990 Great North Run
Newcastle
Half-Marathon
1.06.0.0 (1st)

1990 Dublin Marathon
2.18.4.0 (1st)

1990 10 km Road Race
Loughborough
32.51.0 (1st)

1990 Swiss Nationals
100m   19.3
200m   36.1
400m   1.10.51
800m   2.28.01

1991 World Wheelchair Games
Stoke Mandeville
100m   20.21 (1st)
200m   36.0 (1st)

1991 BWRA National Track Championships *Cwmbran*
100m   18.93
200m   35.03
400m   1.11.7
800m   2.28.1

1991 Welsh Games
Cardiff
100m   21.62
200m   35.83
400m   1.12.35
800m   2.24.86

1992 London Marathon
2.22.23.0 (1st)

1992 St Neots Half-Marathon
1.4.0.0 (2nd)

1992 International Meet
Melbourne
1500m   3.55.96 (6th)
5000m   14.17.7 (5th)

1992 Victoria State Games
200m   33.01 (WR)
800m   2.11.66
5000m   13.37.26

1992 BWRA National Track Championships *Cwmbran*
100m   17.56
200m   33.51
400m   1.08.21
800m   2.25.27
1500m   4.23.35

1992 Metro Toronto Challenge
100m	17.76 (WR)
200m	31.04 (WR)
400m	1.03.00 (WR)
800m	2.05.59 (WR)

1992 Swiss Nationals
Zug
100m	17.76
200m	34.04
400m	1.04.02
800m	2.22.52

1992 Paralympics
Barcelona
100m	17.55 (Gold)
200m	31.19 (Gold)
400m	59.58 (Gold)
800m	2.06.58 (Gold)

1993 Portsmouth Half-Marathon
52.27.0

1993 BWRA National Track Championships
Leicester
100m	17.8
200m	33.0
400m	1.08.1
800m	2.23.5
1500m	4.39.8
5000m	14.59.0
10,000m	27.04.05

1993 World Championships
Stuttgart
800m exhibition
2.01.22 (3rd)

1993 Danish Games
100m	17.2 (1st)
200m	32.28 (1st)
400m	1.07.6 (1st)
800m	2.17.13 (2nd)
1500m	4.14.56 (1st)
5000m	14.12.06 (2nd)
10,000m	26.42.6 (2nd)

1993 Swiss Nationals
Nottwil
100m	17.35 (WR)
400m	58.9 (WR)

1994 London Marathon
2.08.26.0 (1st)

1994 LA Marathon
1.54.40.0 (3rd)

1994 Mobil 10km
24.02.0

1994 BWRA National Track Championsips
Leicester
100m	17.7
200m	31.5
400m	1.02.4
800m	1.59.6
1500m	4.01.0
5000m	13.19.6
10000m	27.37.7

1994 Sempach Marathon
Switzerland
1.53.47.0 (4th)

1994 Sheffield Half-Marathon
1.02.36.0 (1st)

1994 Peachtree 10km
27.34.0 (3rd)

1994 World Championships
Berlin
100m	17.93 (1st)
200m	30.75 (1st) (WR)
400m	58.25 (1st) (WR)
800m	2.00.23 (1st)
1500m	3.42.89 (6th)
5000m	13.09.54 (6th)
10,000m	26.29.04 (3rd)

1994 European Exhibition Event
Helsinki
2.08.28 (3rd)

1995 Oz Day 10km
28.53.1 (3rd)

1995 Victoria Games
Melbourne
100m	17.5
1500m	3.52.54
5000m	13.03.43

1995 Mobil 10km
3rd   25.47.00

1995 BWRA National Track Championships
Gateshead
100m   18.21
200m   34.36
400m   1.02.96
800m   2.22.3
1500m   4.10.31
5000m   14.13.67
10,000m   31.29.3

1995 Leeds 5km
              15.53.00

1995 Glenrothes 10km
              30.51.00

1995 Oensingen Marathon
Switzerland
              2.04.27.00 (3rd)

1995 Liverpool Track Meet
100m   17.6
200m   32.3
400m   1.03.1
800m   2.06.7
1500m   4.01.4
5000m   15.27.1
10,000m   25.39.6

1995 National Wheelchair Games
Stoke Mandeville
200m   33.6
800m   2.10.6
5000m   14.47.4

1995 Welsh Games
Cardiff
100m   17.62
200m   34.64
400m   1.02.47
800m   2.16.13
1500m   4.12.51
5000m   14.27.10

1995 Swiss Track Meet
Luzern
800m   2.07.18 (3rd)

1995 French Track Meet
200m   32.07
800m   2.01.86

1995 International Games
Stoke Mandeville
100m   18.49
200m   34.37
200m   34.06
400m   1.04.49
800m   2.12.09
5000m   14.42.9

1995 Sheffield Half-Marathon
              57.26.0 (1st)

1995 Metro Toronto Challenge
100m   18.92 (1st)
200m   31.91 (1st)
400m   59.06 (1st)
800m   2.05.68 trial
800m   2.09.63
1500m   3.44.33

1995 Gothenburg World Championships
800m   1.53.35 (WR)

1995 Swiss Nationals
Bulle
100m   18.20
200m   31.29
400m   59.55
800m   2.02.07
1500m   3.57.21
5000m   13.17.92
(Won all events)

1995 Berlin Marathon
              1.58.19.00 (3rd)

1995 Batley 10km
              25.48.00 (1st)

Index